W9-BUI-914

10 TRUE TALES

GREATEST POW ESCAPES

ALLAN ZULLO

SCHOLASTIC INC.

To my youngest grandchildren, Ella and Dash
Gorospe and Jack Manausa, may you find the
strength, courage, and determination to
conquer any challenge, no matter the odds.

—A.Z.

ISBN 978-1-338-57174-5

10 9 8 7 6 5 4 3 2 1   20 21 22 23 24

Printed in the U.S.A.   40
First printing September 2020

Book design by Cheung Tai

CONTENTS

ESCAPE ARTISTS   V

SURVIVAL IN THE GREEN MAZE   1
LIEUTENANT DIETER DENGLER

GOING FOR BROKE   23
CORPORAL JACK ARAKAWA

THE COLDITZ HOME RUN   42
LIEUTENANT AIREY NEAVE

THE WOODEN WARHORSE   58
FLIGHT LIEUTENANT OLIVER PHILPOT

ON A WING AND A PRAYER   79
LIEUTENANT ROBERT "BOB" HOOVER

"WE LIVE TO FIGHT ANOTHER DAY"   100
STAFF SERGEANT RICHARD "DICK" MORRIS

ESCAPE FROM THE LIVING DEAD   118
MAJOR WILLIAM "ED" DYESS

CROSSING THE WIRE OF DEATH   138
LIEUTENANT R. ALEX "ANDY" ANDERSON

THE PROMISED LAND   159
LIEUTENANT GEORGE PURYEAR

THE LONG ROAD HOME   179
SERGEANT JOHN RANSOM

ESCAPE ARTISTS

Throughout our country's history, countless American POWs, or prisoners of war, focused on one goal—to escape and return to their units to fight the enemy once again.

However, the odds of pulling off a successful escape (known as a "home run" during World War II) were extremely bad, especially from high-security POW camps operated under inhumane conditions.

During the Civil War, an estimated 211,000 Union soldiers and 220,000 Confederate troops were prisoners of war—more than in any other conflict fought by Americans. About 30,000 Union and 26,000 Confederate POWs died during their captivity from starvation, illness, and torture. Only 1 percent of all imprisoned soldiers—3,000 Union and a smaller number of rebel troops—successfully escaped.

In Europe during World War II, of the 94,000 captured American troops, just 2 percent—or about 1,880 men—broke out of their prison camp and made it safely back to their units. The odds were much worse for the nearly 30,000 Americans held in Japanese-controlled prison camps, where the death rate topped out at 40 percent. Less than 1 percent of these POWs got away, including the ones who pulled off the only mass escape against the Japanese, which you'll read about in this book.

During the Vietnam War, when 725 American servicemen were captured, not a single one successfully escaped from a North Vietnam POW camp. However, in Laos and South Vietnam, 4 percent, or 30 American captives, broke out of their prisons and reached their units.

Despite the overwhelming likelihood of failure, many POWs were willing to risk torture, solitary confinement, and other severe forms of punishment—including execution—if recaptured during an escape attempt. They felt it was their duty, their obligation, their commitment to at least try, no matter what, to break out and reach friendly forces or a neutral country.

Even those POWs who remained in camp—sometimes because of sickness, cruelty, or starvation—often helped escapers by making fake documents, altering or tailoring uniforms and clothes, stealing tools and food, digging tunnels, creating diversions, and picking locks. These stay-behinds displayed their own brand of courage because they knew they faced severe retaliation for their comrades' escape attempts.

Escapes required meticulous planning, cunning ingenuity, spirited courage, and a dash of luck. Often the easy part was the initial prison-camp breakout. The hard part was trying to sneak through hostile, enemy territory with little or no knowledge of the language or to cross harsh, dangerous terrain for days, even weeks, with little or no food.

Relying on published and unpublished memoirs, oral histories, diaries, newspaper accounts, and military documents, this book features daring escapes by American and Allied servicemen from the Vietnam War back to the Civil War.

Former POW Airey Neave, who broke out from an "inescapable" prison, once described an escaper as "a man who must never admit defeat . . . [and who is] always ready to attempt the unknown to achieve the impossible."

You are about to read ten gripping stories about prisoners of war, including Neave, who did indeed achieve the impossible.

SURVIVAL IN THE GREEN MAZE

Lieutenant Dieter Dengler

Attack Squadron 145, USS *Ranger*, US Navy

A corncob! Dieter Dengler felt a rush of glee when he spotted it on the ground. Never mind that the cob was caked in filth and had no kernels on it. To him it was food.

Not a second went by that he and his six fellow POWs didn't feel pangs of hunger, having been forced to survive for months on only two small lumps of rice a day for the entire group in their unbearable prison camp deep in the jungles of Laos during the Vietnam War. So when Dengler saw that discarded dirty corncob, he scooped it up and ravenously gnawed on it.

Catching him in the act, a guard nicknamed Moron by the prisoners exploded in rage. He snatched the cob from Dengler, flung it into the bushes, and then slammed the butt of his rifle into the face of the famished captive. Dazed and bleeding, Dengler slumped to the ground, thinking, *All this over a disgusting corncob that a pig wouldn't eat.*

Starving was nothing new for Dengler. He experienced constant hunger while growing up in Wildberg, Germany, during and after World War II. Little Dieter and his brothers would go into bombed-out buildings and tear off wallpaper, which his widowed mother boiled for the family's dinner because the wallpaper paste contained nutrients.

War plagued his early childhood, but it spawned a dream. During the Allied bombing of his village, six-year-old Dieter watched from his window with a mixture of horror and fascination as a fighter plane roared by at treetop level. Because the plane's canopy was open, the boy got a good look at the leather-clad pilot. From that moment on, Dieter wanted to fly.

In 1956, when he was 18, he saw an ad in an American magazine seeking new pilots. With the help of a relative in the United States, young Dengler took a ship to New York City, where he lived on the streets for a week until he enlisted in the US Air Force. After his enlistment period was up, he earned his citizenship and a college degree and then joined the US Navy, where he became a fighter pilot in the early days of the Vietnam War.

On February 2, 1966, Dengler revved up his Skyraider—a single-seat, single-engine, propeller-driven attack plane—and took off from the deck of the aircraft carrier USS *Ranger* in his first combat mission over communist-controlled North Vietnam. His plane was one of four on a top secret bombing run near the border with Laos.

About two hours into the mission, antiaircraft fire

ripped into the right side of Dengler's plane. Rocked by an explosion that sent the Skyraider into a death dive, he struggled to maintain control while frantically searching for a place to crash-land. All he could see below was thick, dark green jungle in enemy territory.

At the last moment, he spotted a small clearing, but just before touchdown, the crippled aircraft slammed into a large tree. The Skyraider cartwheeled several times before coming to a crunching stop upside down. Thrown 100 feet from the impact, Dengler was knocked out. When he regained consciousness, he felt fortunate that he was not seriously hurt, although he had injured his left leg. After securing his leg in a splint made out of bamboo and vines, he destroyed his maps and equipment so the enemy—North Vietnamese Army troops, Viet Cong, or soldiers of the Laotian communist organization known as the Pathet Lao—couldn't get their hands on them.

He evaded capture through the night and the next day. On the morning of the second full day, he caught sight of two Skyraiders and two helicopters. With hopes of rescue soaring, Dengler ran to a tiny opening in the jungle, tore off his shirt, and waved it. Jumping up and down and shaking his shirt, Dengler shouted, "Over here! Come here!"

Before the helicopters could land, however, Pathet Lao soldiers emerged from the brush and pounced on him. Grabbing him by the arms, they hauled him deep into the jungle. Any hopes of rescue had vanished. For the next several days, they marched Dengler through the tangled green wilderness. Each night they spread-eagled him on the ground and tied him to four stakes to keep him from escaping. The mosquitoes feasted on him, causing his face to swell so much that he could barely see in the mornings.

One day, Dengler sneaked off but was recaptured a few hours later while he was drinking from a jungle watering hole. For his failed escape attempt, the Pathet Lao tortured him and demanded he sign a document condemning the United States. Although battered and bloodied, Dengler refused. He kept reminding himself of the incredible courage and fortitude shown by his maternal grandfather, Hermann Schnuerle. Shortly before World War II, Schnuerle was publicly humiliated and sentenced to work in a rock mine for a year for being the only person in the village who wouldn't support Nazi dictator Adolf Hitler.

For Dengler's refusal to cooperate, he faced more daily torture. One of the Pathet Lao's favorites was to bind his hands to a rope attached to a water buffalo that, when whipped by his guards, would drag him through villages.

Two weeks after his capture, Dengler was brought to a small camp where six prisoners of war, including two Americans, were being held. Their horrendous appearance—sunken cheeks, dull eyes, diseased gums, festering wounds, ratty clothes—told Dengler that they had been held captive for many months. *That's what I'm going to look like if I don't find a way to escape*, he told himself.

His fellow prisoners introduced themselves and explained to him how they ended up captives. Lieutenant

Duane Martin, 26, of the air force's 38th Air Rescue/Recovery Squad, was copiloting a helicopter on a mission to extract a fighter pilot whose plane was shot down near the North Vietnam-Laos border on September 20, 1965. While the downed pilot was being hoisted up from the crash site, heavy enemy ground fire pummeled the chopper, which then crashed. The crewmen survived the impact but were quickly captured. For an unknown reason, the Pathet Lao took Martin alone to this camp, where he joined the other five prisoners, who had been held for nearly two and a half agonizing years.

At the time of their capture, all five were civilians working for Air America, an airline secretly operated by the CIA, the US spy agency. In September 1963, they were members of a crew aboard a twin-engine cargo plane known as a Gooney Bird. They were preparing to airdrop supplies to local friendly forces when enemy antiaircraft fire struck the plane. Before the plane exploded, killing the pilot and copilot, the five parachuted safely to the ground—and right into the clutches of the Pathet Lao.

Over the years, the five—Prasit Promsuwan, Prasit Thanee, and Phisit Intharathat, all from Thailand; To Yick Chiu, a Hong Kong native known as Y.C. To; and an American, Eugene "Gene" DeBruin—spent time in seven prison camps. DeBruin was physically tough, having grown up on a Wisconsin farm and spent a few years as a "smoke jumper," a specially trained wildland firefighter. A kind and caring man who planned to join the Peace Corps after the war,

DeBruin, 32, shared with fellow prisoners his meager food and, on cold nights, his blanket. He helped pass the time as a POW by teaching the others English.

Going from being a lone prisoner to one of seven had its disadvantages for Dengler. At night in one big cell, the POWs were handcuffed to one another, and their feet were locked in wooden stocks.

Because Dengler was new and spoke with a German accent, it took the other prisoners two weeks before they were convinced he was one of them. "Dieter, we have something to tell you," Phisit said. "Ever since you showed up, we've been sleeping in handcuffs and leg blocks even though we can unlock them."

"What do you mean?" Dengler asked.

"Until we were sure you weren't an enemy spy, we had to be careful. The guards don't know that we made a tiny knife to free our feet from the blocks, and we also made a key that unlocks the cuffs. Months ago, I saw a metal piece from a machine gun clip and picked it up along with a small rock. After the guards had put us back into the foot traps, I straightened out the piece of metal and ground it on the rock. It took me several hours to make a knife the size of my little finger. We took turns using the knife to bore out the openings in the foot traps so we could free our feet without the guards knowing."

"How did you make the key?" Dengler asked.

"One day I found an empty toothpaste tube that a guard had dropped on the ground. We thought this could be quite useful. We used dirt to make a mold of the keyhole for the handcuffs. Then we melted the tube and poured it into the mold. It turned out to be a little large, but I used the small knife to scrape and shape it so it could work with all the cuffs."

"So when I arrived, you deliberately kept your hands and feet locked up because you didn't trust me?" Dengler said.

"We can never be too careful," Phisit replied. "We trust you now."

A month after Dengler arrived, he and his comrades were marched for three days through the jungle and past enemy tanks, gun emplacements, and military installations to Ban Houei Het, a new camp designed for just the seven prisoners. Inside a bamboo stockade, two log cells with thatched roofs housed the POWs. Just outside the fence were four similar structures, including huts for 16 guards, a kitchen, and mess hall. Three guard towers loomed over the compound.

The prisoners never saw any villagers or other Pathet Lao soldiers visit the camp. Although they were isolated deep in the rain forest, they often heard American jets overhead and gunfire in the distance.

Each morning, the guards took the POWs to a nearby stream, where they dumped out their waste buckets. Every three days they were allowed to bathe and wash their clothes. Other than walking around the small 70-foot-by-70-foot fenced-in area in the morning, they had little exercise and were shackled in their cells most of the day. They suffered from tropical diseases such as malaria and recurring bouts of dysentery, which left them dehydrated.

The prisoners were so desperate for food they resorted to eating grasshoppers, crickets, lizards, and chameleons that crawled into their cells at night. Like his comrades, Dengler would wake up each morning and remain still while looking for any insect within reach. Seeing one, he would pounce on it, kill it, and put it in the pile of bugs that the others had caught. Then they would make a fire, cook the insects, and eat them. Occasionally, the POWs would "enjoy" a roasted snake or rat that they had speared with a sharpened bamboo stick.

The size of the portion of rice the POWs received slowly shrank until all they were given was a single handful that they had to share. Knowing they were wasting away, the POWs discussed plans for a July escape when the monsoon season would trigger heavy rains that would obscure their tracks and drown out any noise they might make. To prepare for their breakout, they loosened a large pole in one of the cells by pouring water and urinating on its base and working it back and forth every day for weeks until they could remove it. They also loosened several logs close to the floorboards. As part of their plan, they dug a hole under the bamboo fence, which was next to a guard tower, and covered it up with leaves. Meanwhile, the prisoners studied every detail of the guards' routines and movements.

The POWs planned to escape on July 4 simply because it would be their own personal Independence Day. But near the end of June, Phisit huddled with the other prisoners and told them, "I overheard the guards talking about how they are starving and want to go home to their villages. They're planning to march us into the jungle, shoot us, and tell their superiors we tried to escape."

"We can't wait for the rains," Dengler said. "We need to act now."

The prisoners agreed on a plan: They would sneak out of their cells at 4:00 p.m., when the guards put down their weapons and picked up their evening meals in the kitchen. That would take about two and a half minutes, which meant that was all the time the POWs had to slip out of the stockade, secure the guns, and immobilize the guards.

Dengler's job was to enter the nearest guard hut and grab the three weapons left inside, keep one, and pass the others to Phisit and Thanee. At the same time, Martin needed to run to another hut and secure a Thompson submachine gun. Thanee would unlock the other cell to free the remaining three prisoners.

With Dengler guarding the back door of the mess hall and Phisit and Thanee at the front, the Thais would order the unarmed guards to surrender and then round up the rest, ideally without firing any shots, which would alert nearby villages and the Pathet Lao. The prisoners would put the guards in foot traps and handcuffs and lock them in the cells. Next, the prisoners would gather rice and salt and steal the guards' shoes.

According to the plan, the POWs would hustle to the top

of a nearby ridge and then split into separate teams: Dengler and Martin; Thanee and Promsuwan; and Y.C. and DeBruin. Phisit, a former paratrooper, would flee on his own.

At first, no one wanted to team up with Y.C. because he was the sickest and, at age 40, the oldest, and would slow down his partner. Even Y.C. agreed, admitting, "You'll never make it out with me along."

But even though DeBruin knew it lessened his own chances of a successful escape, he insisted on partnering with Y.C. because the bighearted American wasn't going to leave his Air America crewmate behind. "Listen, you guys," DeBruin told the others, "Y.C. and I will go together, and after we reach the ridge, we'll lie in wait for air contact. If you guys get rescued, make sure someone looks for us."

Despite feeling weak and suffering from malaria or other ailments, the POWs were optimistic. They hoped they would find friendly forces known as the Laotian Rightists or catch the attention of American pilots who daily flew over the area. Otherwise, the escapees would have to trek 150 miles to the Thai border to reach safety.

Phisit gave the Americans tips on finding food in the jungle: "You can eat ferns that grow along the waterways. And figs are good, whether they're green or ripe. The easiest animals to catch and eat are baby green frogs and tadpoles. But watch out for baby black toads. They're poisonous.

"I suggest you head west and travel along the waterways. The Mekong River will take you to Thailand. If you make it across the Thai border, people will help you, especially the monks, so seek refuge at a temple until you can make contact with US forces. If you get rescued in Laos, tell searchers to look for the others along the rivers and streams. Under no circumstances go into a village. You'll be captured, then tortured and likely killed."

On the afternoon of July 29, the prisoners' nerves were on edge because the time had come to launch their breakout. Dengler, Martin, Thanee, and Phisit pulled out the loosened pole and logs and emerged from their locked cell. While Thanee opened the other cell, Dengler squeezed under the stockade fence and quietly entered a hut where he found two Chinese rifles, an American M1 carbine, a full ammunition belt, and several magazines. He handed the Chinese rifles to Phisit and Thanee. Martin snared the submachine gun from another hut.

As the rest of the prisoners crawled out of the hole in the stockade, Dengler, Phisit, and Thanee raced toward the open-air mess hall. Phisit yelled at the guards in Laotian, "Stop! Don't move!"

The startled guards froze for a few seconds and then sprinted in all directions. One of the guards had kept a carbine by his side and fired at Dengler, but missed. Dengler killed him with one shot. *So much for assuming the guards didn't take their weapons with them,* he thought.

Moron, the guard who had beaten Dengler for trying to eat a discarded corncob, charged at him with a machete. Dengler shot Moron and then dropped another machete-wielding guard who was running toward him. Phisit gunned down three guards but the rest fled into the jungle.

Knowing the guards would return with reinforcements, the prisoners hurriedly grabbed what supplies they could and put them in rucksacks. When they divvied up the rice, Dengler and Martin made sure that DeBruin and Y.C. received twice as much as the others. The four, who were barefoot, ran into the thick vegetation. But because they were not used to such exertion, they threw up.

When it became obvious that Y.C. was slowing the other three, DeBruin told Dengler, "Go on, Dieter, go on. See you in the States." Dengler, who was too emotional to say anything, grasped DeBruin's hand, shook it, and then ran off with Martin.

Their bare feet sliced up by thorns, Dengler and Martin— each carrying a rifle and a knife—plodded through the dense green maze of the jungle, surviving on fruits, berries, and their ration of rice. After several days, they found the sole of an old tennis shoe, which they took turns wearing by strapping it onto a foot with rattan. It brought them a few moments of relief.

Without a map or compass and hiking under a thick jungle canopy, it was hard for them to tell if they were heading in the right direction. One day, Dengler pushed the brush aside and spotted several abandoned huts across a creek. They looked familiar—too familiar. *Oh, no!* he thought. *I saw them two days ago! We just walked in a huge circle!* He chose not to tell Martin, whose mind was getting fuzzy from hunger and illness, to spare him the anguish and despair that Dengler was feeling.

After ten days, they came to a big river and rejoiced. "This is our highway to freedom!" Dengler shouted. "This will flow to the Mekong River and take us into Thailand." Despite their fatigue and weakness, they built a raft out of bamboo and vines. The exhausted pair then flopped onto the raft and floated down the river.

About two hours later, they heard a thundering noise up ahead. They yelled in unison, "Waterfall!" Martin rolled off the raft and swam to the bank.

Clutching their two rifles, Dengler jumped into the water and began kicking toward the side. But the powerful current had a strong grip on him and swept him toward the falls. *I'm not going to make it!* Discarding one of the rifles, he kicked with all his might. Only a few feet from going over the rushing cascade, he latched onto a jutting rock. *I'm safe!* Shaking from his close call, Dengler watched the raft tumble 300 feet and smash into smithereens in the churning pool below. They'd thought the river would be their lifesaver, but now they realized it could be their killer.

Struggling to keep hope from burning out, they slowly worked their way down the side of the deafening cascade by crawling over slippery, mossy rocks and gripping vines and branches. By the time they reached the bottom, it was dark, and they were exhausted.

The misery never let up. Drenched by torrential monsoon rains for days, they slogged through knee-deep muck. At night they tied themselves to trees so they wouldn't get swept away by recurring mudslides. In the mornings, they needed bamboo sticks to scrape hundreds of leeches off their slime-covered bodies.

One evening, about two weeks after their escape, they rested in an abandoned homestead of three small huts. The rain had stopped, so they tried to build a fire in a clearing, hoping to signal one of the many Allied planes that criss-crossed the area. But the frail men lacked the strength to vigorously rub bamboo sticks together to ignite kindling. To make the task easier, Dengler sprinkled the tinder with the powder from some of their bullets. The trick worked, and they soon were enjoying a decent campfire.

A short time later, they heard a C-130—a lumbering, four-propeller-powered military transport—rumbling over-head. Dengler and Martin leaped to their feet, lit torches, and set fire to the huts. Almost in disbelief, the men saw the plane circle and release two flares that floated down on tiny parachutes. "They see us! They see us!" Dengler cried in jubilation. "Duane, we're going to be saved!"

Although the plane left, the men assumed it would radio the location for a rescue helicopter to come in the morning. The pair's unbridled joy charged them with renewed energy, and they danced and hugged each other. They were so excited they could barely sleep.

The next morning, they woke up in heavy fog and drizzle, which dampened them physically and emotionally. But once the fog lifted, so did their spirits. The chopper would show up any moment, they figured. However, with each passing hour, their hopes of rescue diminished until they came to the devastating realization that no one was coming to save them.

Distraught, starving, and soaked by another deluge, they tramped onward, seeking the Mekong River. Dengler found a parachute from one of the flares draped over a bush. Stuffing it in his rucksack, he told Martin, "This should come in handy."

On the eighteenth day, they followed a trail, and when it crested a hill, they saw a hamlet below. Throughout their escape, they had avoided detection by skirting all the villages they had neared. But driven by the madness of hunger, Martin said, "Dieter, I'm going down there to steal some food."

"Are you crazy?" Dengler replied. "That's a sure way to get killed."

"I'm going anyway."

This is not a good idea, Dengler thought, *but I can't let Duane go alone*. Walking down the trail, they encountered a little boy, who screamed and ran off when he saw two scruffy white men in tattered clothes.

Suddenly, a villager with a machete approached the Americans. They dropped to their knees and held their hands in prayer, signaling they were no threat. Dengler laid down his rifle. Whether out of fear or hatred of Americans, the man raised his machete and swung at Dengler, who ducked. The machete missed him by a few inches but struck Martin in the thigh.

Martin shrieked in pain. Dengler screamed in terror.

Before either could move, the man slashed Martin again, this time with a fatal blow. "Nooo!" Dengler bellowed. Enraged, he sprang to his feet and tackled the attacker, but the man squirmed free. Dengler picked up his rifle, scrambled off the trail, and hid in the brush while villagers looked for him briefly before giving up their search.

Later, from a high vantage point, he caught a glimpse of a squad of Viet Cong soldiers who were tracking him, so he scampered along a path until he reached a fork. While wondering which way to go, he saw a vision of his father, a German soldier who had died in battle in World War II when Dengler was an infant. The vision looked exactly like the only possession he had of his dad—a photo of him in uniform—and it was pointing in the direction of a bluff overlooking a river. Without hesitating, Dengler ran toward the bluff. Climbing over rocks, he hid from view and watched with relief as the soldiers took the other fork. "Thank you, Father," he murmured.

Still in shock over losing his friend, Dengler wobbled along the riverbank as if he were a walking corpse—which, in a way, he was. He had reached the point where he didn't much care if he lived or died.

His feeble, bony body—clad only in a torn shirt and pants frayed to his upper thighs—was blemished with scratches, sores, and scabs from head to toe. The rifle felt as though it weighed a hundred pounds. *Maybe I should just chuck it.* That night, he decided to give up. *I'm not taking another step*, he told himself. *I'm going to lie here in the jungle and starve to death.*

The next morning, his survival instincts kicked in, and he continued to hike, motivated in part by a bear he saw following him. *He's just waiting for me to die so he can eat me.* The bear, its smooth black fur glistening from a rain shower, tailed him for two days. At times when Dengler was feeling sorry for himself, he considered the animal a pet, thinking, *It's the only friend I have.* But the weary escapee realized the bear represented death—his own.

Worn out mentally and physically, Dengler began to hallucinate. He had trouble determining what was real and what was imaginary. While crawling along the riverbed, he looked up and saw two enormous doors in front of him. When they opened up, horses ridden by heavenly angels galloped out. In Dengler's unhinged mind, they were not angels of death but angels of faith, which could only mean one thing: *Death doesn't want me.*

On July 20—five days after Martin's murder and 23 days after fleeing the prison camp—Dengler was planning to rest on a boulder by a river bend when he slipped, fell, and landed on a rock where a brilliantly colored snake was coiled. Because hunger had overtaken any sense of caution, Dengler grabbed the snake by its head without caring if it was poisonous or not. Stretching it out by the tail, the famished escapee bit the snake in two and ate half of it. He stuffed the rest in his pocket.

And then he heard a familiar sound. *Could it be? Could it really be?* He looked up. *It is!* Two Skyraiders, one high and one low, were flying over the river. Dengler began waving his arms as the low-flying plane flew past. "No, don't leave!" Dengler cried out.

Hoping against hope the planes would return, he ripped off his shirt and pants, yanked the little parachute from his rucksack, and spread them out to form an SOS on the rock. Minutes later, he heard the Skyraiders. *Am I hallucinating?* When they made another pass, he knew his imagination was not playing tricks. *This is real!*

Dengler picked up the parachute and began twirling it over his head. "Oh, God, please don't let them leave me this time! Please! Please!"

Noticing a waterway that cut through the impenetrable Laotian jungle, Lieutenant Colonel Gene Deatrick radioed his wingman, Major Andy Anderson. "You stay high while I drop down and follow this river."

The two were flying their US Air Force A-1 Skyraiders on a mission for the 1st Air Commando Squadron, looking to strike any enemy targets they saw. When Deatrick banked his plane, he looked down and glimpsed a man jumping up and down on a rock outcropping at a bend in the river. "Hey, Andy, I just saw some nut waving at me."

The pilots laughed. Deatrick continued on his low-level curvy flight path, but something didn't seem right. "Andy, I'm going back to make another pass," he radioed. "Laotians in hostile territory don't wave at American planes."

Anderson tailed him, and on their return, they saw a skinny, almost naked man frantically signaling them with something white. "Whoever it is, it looks like he made an SOS, minus the O," Anderson said.

The two pilots circled overhead while Deatrick contacted the region's airborne command-and-control center and asked, "Has anyone been shot down in the area?"

"Negative," came the reply. "No Air Force, no Navy, no Marine, no Thai."

"Well, someone is down there, and he's definitely trying to get our attention," Deatrick said.

"It couldn't be a downed pilot," the controller replied.

Deatrick kept insisting that the person beckoning them was a friendly who deserved to get rescued. His persistence finally paid off, and headquarters agreed to dispatch two helicopters. When they neared the site, Deatrick escorted the lead chopper to the site.

"That guy better not be a Viet Cong," Anderson radioed Deatrick.

"I know," Deatrick replied. "If he is, he might blow up the chopper and kill everyone aboard as well as my military career."

Two helicopters arrived, and one positioned itself over Dengler. Putting on his clothes, Dengler kept reminding himself he wasn't hallucinating. *This is really happening!* As the jungle penetrator, a device that looks like a three-armed anchor, was lowered by winch and cable from the hovering helicopter, Dengler heard a shot echoing along the river. And then another one. He knew who was firing. The Viet Cong trackers had spotted the helicopters and were intent on thwarting the rescue. Now it was a race between the Americans and the enemy troops, who were still several hundred yards away.

"Hurry! Hurry!" yelled Dengler.

When the penetrator reached him, he draped his armpits over the prongs of the device and gave a thumbs-up. Meanwhile, enemy bullets flew as crewmen aboard both choppers returned fire. Gripping the penetrator, Dengler closed his eyes, praying he wouldn't get shot. *Not like this. Not when I'm so close.*

Suddenly, he felt two firm hands seize him and pull him inside the helicopter. When Dengler opened his eyes, he stared into the face of air force pararescue specialist Michael Leonard. Wrapping his thin arms around Leonard's leg, Dengler wept.

Fearing that Dengler might be a suicide bomber, Leonard, who weighed more than 250 pounds, pinned him to the flight deck while two rescue specialists examined the rucksack and stripped off Dengler's clothes looking for any explosive device.

Pulling the half-eaten snake out of Dengler's pocket, one of the crewmen yelped and instinctively leaped backward, nearly falling out of the chopper's open door. After recovering, he announced, "Nothing on him." Turning to Dengler, he then asked, "Who are you?"

"I am a US Navy pilot who was shot down," Dengler replied between sobs. "Please take me home. I want to go home."

Dieter Dengler, who was missing for nearly five months, was close to death when he arrived at the hospital, according to doctors. He weighed only 98 pounds and suffered from malaria, intestinal worms, fungus, and hepatitis. But he made a full recovery.

Awarded the Navy Cross, Distinguished Flying Cross, Bronze Star, Air Medal, and Purple Heart, Dengler left the navy in 1968, settled near San Francisco, and became a civilian test pilot before flying for a commercial airline. Dengler, who wrote a book about his captivity called Escape from Laos, *was married three times and had two children. In 2001—almost 35 years to the day of his capture—he died at age 62 and was buried with full military honors in Arlington Cemetery.*

Of the other POWs who escaped with him, Gene DeBruin was reportedly recaptured but was never heard from again. There was no word of the fates of Y.C. To, Prasit Promsuwan, and Prasit Thanee. Phisit Intharathat was on the run for 32 days before he was recaptured and held in a different POW camp. Five months later, he and 52 other prisoners were rescued in a raid by American special forces. He returned to work for Air America until the end of the war in 1975 and then settled in Bangkok, Thailand.

Dengler's book and Intharathat's firsthand account were major sources for this chapter.

GOING FOR BROKE

Corporal Jack Arakawa

Company C, 19th Infantry Regiment, 24th
Infantry Division, US Army

OW Jack Arakawa had just finished helping bury the bodies of six fellow American soldiers—all victims of cruelty at the hands of their communist North Korean captors—when he heard heartening news from a villager.

"The First Cavalry and the First Infantry are winning south of here and should reach this area by the end of the week," revealed the Korean, a Christian who sided with Americans. "The North Korean soldiers are panicking and in full retreat."

"That's great," said Arakawa. "We'll soon be freed from all this misery."

The villager, an elderly man wearing a cross around his neck, shook his head and said, "There's more. I was told all you prisoners will be moved out tonight and marched to Manchuria."

Referring to the desolate region in neighboring

communist China, Arakawa said, "But the border is a hundred miles away. Most of us are too weak and sick to make it. We're losing six to eight men a day in prison."

Turning to his four comrades who, along with him, had been handling burial duty for the last several days, Arakawa whispered, "When the First Cavalry arrives, we'll all be gone—or dead. We have to escape tonight."

"But how?" asked one of his fellow POWs.

Replied Arakawa, "I have a plan."

Born and raised in Hawaii, the stocky 29-year-old soldier earned his reputation as a fierce fighter throughout World War II in the highly decorated 442nd Regimental Combat Team, an army unit composed of Japanese Americans. He lived by the unit's motto, "Go for Broke," which is gambler's slang for risking everything in an all-out effort to win big. As a machine gunner who fought off a German patrol while wounded in France in 1944, Arakawa earned a Bronze Star—a combat medal for valor—and a Purple Heart.

Six years later, on July 2, 1950, Arakawa arrived in South Korea with his new unit—Company C, 19th Infantry Regiment, 24th Infantry Division—to help defend the country against the invading troops from communist North Korea known as the Korean People's Army (KPA). The United States was part of the United Nations Command, a coalition of forces from 16 countries, led by US general Douglas

MacArthur. American soldiers were fighting alongside their Republic of Korea counterparts, trying to save ill-prepared, beleaguered South Korea.

On July 16, two weeks after stepping onto Korean soil, the battle-hardened machine gunner and his comrades set up defensive positions near the South Korean town of Taejon (now Daejeon). When enemy tanks rumbled toward them that evening, the outnumbered Americans unleashed their firepower, but it wasn't enough to slow the advancing KPA soldiers.

His commander ordered his besieged unit to withdraw. Despite enduring heavy small-arms fire and blasts from nearby mortar rounds, Arakawa remained behind to lay down cover for the retreating Americans. But then his weapon jammed and exploded, leaving him blind and deaf for several minutes. When he recovered, he picked up a Browning automatic rifle from a fallen soldier and continued firing, enabling the rest of his comrades to evacuate. Before he had a chance to flee, however, a KPA bullet struck his weapon's clip and grazed his chest, knocking him out.

When Arakawa regained consciousness, he discovered he was alone behind enemy lines. He slinked off undetected into the hills, but when he reached a nearby village where he hoped to hide, he was captured by a North Korean patrol. As they tied his wrists together with wire, he recalled the horror stories he'd heard about the enemy's fondness for executing bound American captives. *I'm a dead man*, he thought.

As far as the army was concerned, Arakawa *was* dead. Seeing him be shot and drop, his retreating comrades had reported him killed in action. The army sent an official notification of death to his wife, Lia, who was caring for their two children, Jack, four, and Marylou, three, back home in Honolulu. General MacArthur even wrote a letter of condolence to Lia, whose in-laws arranged for memorial services in Hawaii to honor their son.

But Arakawa was not dead. Because he was Asian and had some knowledge of the Korean language, he was spared. When he told his captors he was an American, they didn't believe him, but eventually he convinced them he was from Hawaii. "If you work hard, we will send you home in a plane after the war," a KPA officer told him. "If you don't work hard, we will send you home in a box."

Several guards still assumed Arakawa was a North Korean traitor because of his Asian features and short hair. (South Korean soldiers wore their hair much longer than KPA troops did.) Condemning him for being an Asian fighting for the "white imperialists," the guards harassed him by firing bullets at his feet while he stood at attention.

However, the KPA officers considered Arakawa an asset because he acted as an interpreter for the other prisoners. In fact, the officers tried to lure him to their side. "If you join the KPA, you will attain great heights and be part of a strong machine fighting for the good of all mankind," an officer told him. "After we win the war, you will be rewarded with a house and servants, better food, sake, medical care, and parties."

Arakawa declined the offer. Over the next six weeks, as the KPA kept pushing deeper into South Korea, his captors forced him and hundreds of other prisoners to lug ammunition and hefty sacks of rice at gunpoint. Weighted down by their heavy loads, the captives labored as human pack mules day after day. At night, the POWs were bound by their wrists and ordered to sleep next to the ammo stockpile, so they would surely die if the unit was attacked or bombed.

What passed for food—fly-ridden rice and dried fish teeming with worms—wasn't enough to sustain a healthy body. Arakawa pleaded with his captors to provide weary prisoners with edible food, decent rest, and medical care, but the inhumane treatment continued. To taunt the prisoners, guards raided farms for chickens and vegetables and ate their plunder in front of them.

In early September, Arakawa and his fellow POWs were confined in a prison camp converted from a former school in Seoul, the enemy-occupied capital of South Korea. There, guards tried to brainwash the POWs daily, asking such questions as, "How could you admire President Truman when he killed two hundred thousand innocent people?" (This was a reference to Truman's order to drop two atomic bombs on Japan, effectively ending World War II.) Prisoners attended mandatory lectures on the evils of Wall Street capitalism and the righteousness of the North Korean cause. They had to watch propaganda films contrasting racial prejudice in the United States with the "ideal life" of the communist world.

At the prison, Arakawa became friends with Private First Class Edward "Grady" Halcomb, a lanky 19-year-old medic from Company B, 1st Battalion, 29th Infantry Regiment. They often chatted during breaks while picking the lice off their filthy clothes.

Halcomb, of Hamilton, Ohio, recalled that on July 26, 1950, his battalion was attacked in the town of Anui. "My unit was annihilated," he said. "By one o'clock in the mornin', there were just eleven of us left, and we were makin' our last stand inside a schoolhouse. The North Koreans were throwin' grenades down the hallway, and we were pickin' 'em up and throwin' 'em back. That was no fun. And it sure as heck wasn't no fun gettin' shot in the shoulder and leg. Just flesh wounds is all. Well, we finally ran out of ammo and surrendered. So that was a bad break.

"Later that mornin', they took our nice, pretty combat boots from us and gave us their own small beat-up shoes." Halcomb pointed to his exposed toes, which were sticking out of a pair of ratty canvas shoes. "I had to cut the fronts out of 'em so my feet can fit. That's why my toes are hangin' out like this. There're a lot of us walkin' 'round this way. Another bad break.

"Then when reinforcements of the good guys started pushin' the enemy backward, the North Koreans brought us to Seoul and this lovely place."

By now, the POW camp held 376 Americans, many of them suffering from malnutrition, illness, and untreated combat wounds. As the senior medic in the group, Halcomb had set up a sick room and, with limited supplies, tended to the medical needs of his fellow captives. "That's a lot of what keeps me goin'," he told Arakawa. "I know I have a responsibility as the senior medic to look after the men."

Two months after his capture, Arakawa overheard guards talking about how American-led troops had invaded the port city of Incheon on September 15 and were now heading toward Seoul. "Maybe good luck is coming our way," Arakawa told Halcomb. "Our boys are about to kick the North Koreans out of Seoul and free us."

But the KPA dashed his hopes when guards were getting ready to march all the POWs to the North Korean capital of Pyongyang 120 miles away. On September 21, while South Korean forces launched an attack to recapture Seoul in fierce street fighting, armed KPA guards ushered the POWs out of the city.

And so began a brutal death march. Walking about 10 miles a day in bitter cold, the weary prisoners—many of them barefoot, bloodied, and suffering from maggot-infested wounds—were often denied water and given little food. Once a day, each was fed a small clump of rice the size of a tennis ball. When the march halted every two to three hours for a break, the men weren't even allowed to sit. The POWs started falling by the wayside, one by one. The guards shot or bayoneted those who couldn't keep up, and left the victims' bodies where they lay in the streets, along roadside ditches, and on mountain trails. Halcomb did all he could to help the weak. Arakawa kept urging the slowest ones not to give up, and so did Major William "Tom" McDaniel, Sr., the highest-ranking officer among the prisoners.

An average of six to ten men a day were dying on the death march. If disease, injuries, starvation, or beatings didn't claim lives, friendly fire did. It happened after McDaniel convinced the guards to allow the sickest prisoners to ride in oxcarts. The major gave Halcomb the responsibility of choosing who rode in the carts. On the morning of October 4, 15 oxcarts were about a mile from the main group of POWs when the pilot of an American fighter jet mistook those in and around the carts as the enemy and strafed them, killing 11 prisoners. Several times, pilots of other American planes wrongly assumed the POW column was of retreating KPA soldiers and shot at them.

McDaniel ordered his men to position themselves in a formation that spelled F-O-O-D, which could only be seen by American pilots flying overhead. Eventually, the US Air Force realized the marchers were POWs and dispatched a C-47 cargo plane that dropped cases of food rations by parachute to them. The starving prisoners broke ranks and scrambled to pick up the coveted canned meals scattered over the area. But the guards took all the rations away, claiming they would pass out the food to the POWs the next day. They lied. The following morning, the prisoners discovered their captors had stolen and eaten the food.

After crossing into North Korea, the glum prisoners were paraded through villages where residents jeered and threw garbage at them. By the time the POWs had reached Pyongyang after the 14-day death march, nearly half had died. The survivors were put into another prison that had once been a school. Halcomb worked tirelessly to treat his ailing comrades, but without any medical supplies, he couldn't stem the increasing death rate.

With Arakawa acting as the interpreter, McDaniel tried to negotiate for more medicine, water, and food. The KPA prison commandant scoffed at the request, telling the American, "You and your men are getting the same amount of food as our own soldiers, so why would we give you any more than what we get?"

The prison camp was guarded by trigger-happy sentries eager to shoot anyone who neared the perimeter fence. The commandant made it clear that if anyone tried to escape, their leader, Major McDaniel, would be executed.

The only POWs allowed to leave the camp under armed guard were members of the five-man burial detail. The major had arranged with the commandant to bury dead POWs in the nearby cemetery of a Christian church.

Arakawa and Halcomb joined Sergeants William H. Jones, of Flint, Michigan, and Robert L. Morris, of Chester, Pennsylvania, on the burial detail commanded by Lieutenant Jimmy Smith, of Columbus, Ohio, a member of the famed African American unit known as the Tuskegee Airmen. Although burying the dead was grim work, Arakawa and the others were grateful to spend a few hours outside the prison. Before each burial, Smith led the group in a simple prayer and then placed next to the body a bottle that contained a piece of paper with the victim's name, rank, serial number, and date of death.

On October 14, the group had just finished burying the last of six dead Americans when an elderly man from the church approached Arakawa. The man told him the United States' 1st Cavalry Division and South Korea's 1st Infantry Division had the KPA soldiers on the run and, at the present pace, were likely to reach Pyongyang in five days. When asked how he knew this, the man replied, "This message was passed from village to village."

However, with the good news came the bad news—the surviving POWs would be moving, probably by another death march, to a prison at the Manchurian border. "There's no way we can make it," Arakawa told his comrades. "We've lost nearly two hundred men since we left Seoul. And the rest of us are barely hanging on. If we are to survive, we need to escape. It's time we go for broke."

"But how?" asked Halcomb.

After giving the question some thought, Arakawa replied, "I have a plan. But Lieutenant Smith and I have to run it by Major McDaniel first. Remember what the commandant said. He'd kill McDaniel if anyone escaped. But if my plan works, they won't know we're missing. It's really very basic—and very risky."

"Heck, we might as well die tryin'," said Halcomb. "It's

better than dyin' without tryin'." Turning to Smith, Jones, and Morris, he asked, "You boys in?" When they nodded, he grinned and, echoing Arakawa, said, "Let's go for broke."

When the five Americans returned to the camp, Arakawa and Smith told McDaniel of their escape plan. "Go ahead," the major told him. "And Godspeed."

"Sir, why don't you come with us," Smith said. "You're not in quite as bad shape as most, so . . ."

The major cut him off and replied, "No, I need to stay here with my men. It's my duty. Besides, if they found out I was missing, there would be an all-out manhunt for me, which would lower your chances of success. And there's another important reason I must remain with my men: I hope to stop any more beatings and killings."

"But what about the commandant's threat to kill you if anyone escapes?" Arakawa asked.

"That's not your concern." Shaking hands with Arakawa and Smith, the major said, "Just don't get caught. Good luck."

That night, the prisoners lined up in rows, four abreast, with armed guards at the head and the rear. Arakawa and the other four from the burial detail stayed together near the front of the column. As the prisoners moved out, he whispered to his comrades, "It's now or never."

They marched down an unlit street lined with shuttered shops and ramshackle houses. As they passed a darkened alley that separated two buildings, Smith slipped out of the column and into the alley, followed by the other four. They hurriedly and quietly hustled down the alley—and ran straight into a 20-foot-tall wall. "A dead end?" Arakawa fumed in a low voice. "Of all the rotten luck."

"Fall back into the column before it passes us by," Smith said. "We'll try again."

Having tasted a minute of freedom, they all dreaded returning to the march, but they did anyway, merging with the group without the guards noticing them. After walking 50 yards, they passed another alley between two shops. Once again, the men peeled away from the column and into the alley, which was a block long. Rather than risk exposure on the other side where residents might see them, the escapees pressed themselves against the wall of one of the buildings and waited for the POWs and guards to pass them by.

None of the five said anything, but they all thought the same thing: *If we're caught now, they will execute us.* After remaining still for half an hour, the five ventured out and headed for the south end of the city. They repeatedly had to duck behind bushes, houses, and buildings to avoid being seen by the growing number of residents who were fleeing before the American and South Korean forces arrived for a showdown with the KPA.

Along the way, the escapees picked up discarded empty glass bottles and deliberately broke them, turning the jagged edges into weapons. They also fashioned crude knives out of wood scraps lying on the ground. Their best discovery was a torn KPA uniform shirt dangling from a clothesline. "Luck is on our side," Arakawa said, putting it on. "Now I look like a North Korean soldier who's marching my prisoners."

"But to pull that off, you need a rifle," Halcomb said. "How are you gonna get one?"

"Here's how," said Smith, walking over to a tree. He snapped a six-foot-long limb off a thick branch, broke it in half over his knee, and said, "Here's your weapon, Jack. From far away at night, it could pass for a rifle."

Arakawa rested the limb over his shoulder and said, "Okay, you prisoners. March!" With his four comrades walking in front of him, Arakawa acted like a gruff North Korean guard, occasionally barking in Korean, *"Pali-pali!"* ("Hurry up!") whenever a resident spotted them.

Around 4:00 a.m., they reached the outskirts of the city, where police were manning a major roadblock. On either side stretched three-foot-high barriers made of cement and iron. "How are we going to get past that?" Halcomb asked.

"Can you bluff your way?" Smith asked Arakawa.

Arakawa shook his head. "My Korean isn't that good, and without a real rifle, there's no way I can fake it."

"Well, we can't just hang around here," said Halcomb. "It'll be daylight soon."

After giving it some thought, Arakawa said, "Let's go for broke." He then explained his idea to the others. It was a long shot, but at this point they had no other options. They agreed to go ahead with his do-or-die plan.

All five were taking deep breaths to keep their nerves in check as they marched directly toward the guarded lit-up roadblock. They pulled the broken bottles and wooden knives out of their pockets in preparation for possible hand-to-hand combat. Nearing the lighted area but still shrouded in darkness, the escapees broke out into a mad dash as Arakawa hollered, *"Gongseub! Gongseub!"* ("Air raid! Air raid!")

Just as he had hoped, the guards scattered to the left and right. The Americans charged the roadblock and leaped over the barriers. Catching a glimpse of the escapees rushing past them under the lights, the guards realized they had been duped. By the time the guards began shooting, the Americans had disappeared into the darkness.

The five kept running as fast as their wobbly, weakened legs could carry them. The guards made a half-hearted effort to chase them, but quickly gave up.

When the escapees stopped to catch their breath, Smith told the others, "We need to find a place to hide—and soon. It's almost daybreak."

They went door to door in search of a vacant house, and finally found one just as the morning light overtook the night. Forcing open the back door, they entered a small three-room home that showed signs the occupants had abandoned it in a hurry. In the kitchen area, they found a sack of flour, another one of rice, a bag of sesame seeds, three apples, and a large container of water.

As the light grew brighter, they peeked out the window and noticed the house sat on a fairly busy street in a neighborhood of warehouses and homes. Residents carrying large bags on their backs or pulling carts loaded with furniture and other possessions were evacuating the city. "We'll stay put right here," Smith told the others. "No one goes near the window during the day or goes out at night. We can't risk being seen. We have food and water for a few days, so we'll sit tight and hope that the First Cavalry shows up before we run out of supplies."

The next morning, Smith glanced out the window and saw a North Korean man leaning against a building across the street, staring at the house. The man didn't leave until later in the afternoon. He showed up again the following day, and the day after that. "I don't know what he's doing there, but if he's a spy, he would have alerted the KPA by now," Smith said.

On the fourth day of holing up, the escapees heard the distant sound of explosions and American bombers flying overhead. Outside, more people hauling possessions were scurrying down the street. "It won't be long now," Smith said.

"I'm goin' stir-crazy," Halcomb admitted. The men tried to pass the time talking about their upbringing, their families, and their plans for the future when—or if—they returned home. At the others' insistence, Arakawa and Smith recalled their World War II combat experiences.

On the fifth day, October 20, with their food and water almost gone, the escapees began hearing shouts of "Manse! Manse!" Arakawa took a quick glimpse out the window. The man across the street was smiling at a young couple. He raised his arms with his palms facing toward each other (like a football referee signaling a field goal).

"Jack, can you tell what's going on?" Smith asked.

"They're cheering," Arakawa replied. "They're saying 'Hooray.' Many North Korean folks would welcome the Americans. Of course, there are many who support the KPA. So either the American and South Korean troops have entered the city or the KPA has defeated them. Sir, I request permission to talk to the man and find out."

After a lengthy hesitation, Smith agreed, adding, "I'm betting on the Americans."

Feeling somewhat apprehensive, Arakawa left the house and walked over to the man and the couple, who were now pointing in his direction. He turned around to see what they were looking at. When he saw it, he smiled and relaxed. Draped over the side of a warehouse behind the house was a big South Korean flag. *That could mean only one thing,* he thought. *The Americans and South Koreans have arrived.*

When he talked to the trio, they confirmed that the 1st Cavalry and 1st Infantry Divisions had indeed captured Pyongyang. Later in the conversation, Arakawa asked the old man, "Why were you staring at the house for the last five days?"

The man replied, "I was waiting to see the South Korean flag go up."

Arakawa and his four comrades were soon surrounded by happy, backslapping 1st Infantry soldiers, who congratulated them on their escape. The former POWs were then whisked off to headquarters of the 1st Cavalry, where they met three other escapees from the same prison camp—Captain William Locke, of Enfield, North Carolina; Lieutenant Alexander Makarounis, of Lowell, Massachusetts; and Sergeant Takeshi "Tak" Kumagai, of Honolulu, Hawaii. The three said a Christian North Korean who worked in the prison camp helped them escape. He knew of a trapdoor in the floor of a room that opened into a small chamber. Shortly before all the POWs were moved out, the trio hid under the floor until their friend told them it was safe to come out.

Like his comrades, Arakawa was skin and bones, having gone from 160 to 120 pounds during his 97 days in captivity. (Halcomb had lost 50 pounds.) For the first time in months, the eight former POWs ate and drank to their heart's content—and promptly suffered stomach problems. But Arakawa didn't mind. He told the others, "It's a small price to pay to celebrate our freedom."

On October 14, 1950, the day when the eight Americans escaped, the remaining 180 POWs were marched through Pyongyang to the train station and loaded into open railroad cars. Later the next day, they began a slow ride northward toward the Manchurian border. Already weakened by the Seoul-Pyongyang death march, they rode unprotected in the wintry weather for five days. Many died along the way from disease, exposure, and lack of food, water, and medical care.

On October 20, the train stopped at a tunnel near Sunchon, North Korea. In groups of 40, the prisoners were taken off the train and to a ravine where they were told they would be fed. Instead, the North Koreans opened fire, slaughtering them, including Major Tom McDaniel. Incredibly, 22 POWs who were shot managed to survive by playing dead. They were found the next day by advancing American forces.

Out of the original 376 POWs in Arakawa's group who started out together in the death march from Seoul, only 30 returned home alive—including the "dead" Jack Arakawa.

He had no idea he had been officially listed as killed in action. Nor did he know that he had been "posthumously" awarded the Silver Star—a prestigious combat medal for valor—for his courageous actions near Taejon when he was "killed."

"I never wanted to believe that Jack was dead," his wife, Lia, told reporters when she received word that he was alive. Even after her letters to him were returned with "DECEASED" stamped on them, she still had held out hope.

Arakawa reenlisted twice and completed his military career in 1964 as a staff sergeant with the 8th Army in Korea. He returned to his native Hawaii, where he worked as a cargo clerk at Hickam Air Force Base until his death in 1973 at age 52.

Grady Halcomb remained in the army for 20 years and

then moved to Florida, where he owned and operated a service station and a bait-and-tackle shop before retiring to Mulberry, Florida. In 2016, after a delay of 66 years and an act of Congress, Halcomb, then 84, was awarded the Distinguished Service Cross—the second highest award for valor—for his efforts in trying to keep his fellow POWs alive under horrific conditions. The nomination for the award had been lost during the war. It was uncovered by Colonel Tom McDaniel, Jr., while doing research for a book he was writing about his late father, who posthumously earned the Distinguished Service Cross for "his courage and his unwavering devotion to duty and his men."

The citation for Halcomb's medal said, "By placing himself with the most disabled, PFC Halcomb increased the probability of his own execution as the enemy guards executed [fellow American POWs], whose physical condition became a burden or slowed the pace." Too overwhelmed by the honor and the gut-wrenching memories, Halcomb had one of his daughters accept the honor "on behalf of all the boys and all the young men" who didn't survive being prisoners of war.

THE COLDITZ HOME RUN

Lieutenant Airey Neave

1st Searchlight Regiment, Royal Artillery,
British Army

When Lieutenant Airey Neave first stepped foot in his latest POW camp, he let out a low whistle of awe. *Oh, boy,* he thought, *it's not going to be easy to escape from this place.*

Officially known as Oflag IV-C, the high-security prison was actually an 800-year-old fortress known as Colditz Castle, which looked out over the town with the same name in eastern Germany. Built with seven-foot-thick outer walls, the castle sat on a cliff that dropped 250 feet to the Mulde River below. More than 70 German soldiers and officers patrolled the sprawling grounds. Because the Nazis considered it escape-proof, the camp held hundreds of captured Allied officers, many known as *Ausbrecher*—prisoners who had attempted escapes from other camps.

Neave was one such POW. At the outbreak of World War II, the Oxford-educated lawyer enlisted in the British military and was deployed with the 1st Searchlight Regiment of the Royal Artillery. As a 24-year-old officer, he was fighting against the Germans when he was badly wounded during a battle in Calais, France, in May 1940. While he was lying in the cellar of a French hospital, the area came under heavy shellfire. Despite his injuries, he pushed aside nurses who tried to restrain him and staggered out of the building to help his comrades. But he eventually collapsed and was captured on the evening of May 26 while he lay on a stretcher.

After nearly three months in a hospital, he was sent to Oflag IX-A, a POW camp in the heart of Germany. He spent seven months there before being shipped off to Stalag XX-A, a huge complex in Thorn (now Toruń), Poland, that housed about 10,000 prisoners. Sanitary conditions and food were deplorable. Prisoners, who were required to stand at attention three times a day during *appell* (roll call), were locked in underground, windowless rooms from 8:00 p.m. to 7:00 a.m. every day. Guards beat POWs with clubs for any infraction of the rules, no matter how slight.

Neave was fed up with the mistreatment. On April 16, 1941, less than two months after his arrival at Stalag XX-A, he sneaked out of the camp dressed as a German officer. He hoped to reach Soviet-occupied territory in Poland. While on the run in the country's German-held territory, he noticed that the Nazis had destroyed crucifixes and religious monuments. He witnessed members of the Hitler Youth, a Nazi-inspired organization of 14- to 18-year-olds, beat up Polish Jews while pro-German onlookers cheered.

Relying on the kindness of anti-Nazi Poles, he had

managed to travel 90 miles from the prison camp before he was captured. Because he was considered an *Ausbrecher,* he was sent to Colditz, arriving there on May 14, 1941.

Unlike in other POW camps, the Wehrmacht—the armed forces of Nazi Germany—followed the Geneva Convention to the letter and treated prisoners decently in Colditz. Guards knew it was the duty of the POWs to try to escape and treated them with respect. In fact, some prisoners made gentlemen's agreements with the guards not to use borrowed tools for escape attempts in return for special privileges. During the war, the castle—which in previous decades had been a zoo, a mental institution, a sanitarium, and a workhouse for the poor—held more than 500 captives, including prominent Jews and political prisoners.

In addition to the guards, the castle grounds bustled with civilians and local townspeople. These included maintenance workers, medics, observers from the Swiss Red Cross, Nazi Party leaders, and family members of the military officers at the camp.

The Wehrmacht allowed POWs to come up with their own forms of entertainment. Polish prisoners organized the first camp Olympics, which included soccer, volleyball, boxing, and chess. For fun and to work out aggression, POWS played a game they created called stool ball—a brutal offshoot of rugby where a team scores a point every time it knocks the opposing team's goalie off a stool.

Prisoners formed a Polish choir, a Dutch Hawaiian guitar band, and a French orchestra to entertain their comrades as well as the guards. The British produced plays, talent shows, and farces at the camp theater. Several prisoners loved acting so much they intentionally grew their hair long so they could better portray women. Guards allowed POWs to use tools and paint to build sets for their productions with the promise that the items wouldn't be used for escape attempts. To make better use of their time, officers from different countries taught each other their languages.

To find out what was happening in the war, prisoners couldn't rely on letters from family because they were screened by censors, and the German newspapers delivered in camp were filled with lies and Nazi propaganda. However, the prisoners secretly listened to BBC broadcasts on a radio that was smuggled into the castle and kept hidden from the guards. The British War Office communicated with POWs in code on certain radio programs and also sent escape aids concealed in care packages from families and fake charities.

Red Cross boxes were not touched by the war office out of concern the Germans would ban them from all prison camps. But the prisoners often swapped items from those same boxes with guards and townspeople for information, tools, and money for use in escape attempts.

To curb breakouts, guards held three to four *appells* a day to count the prisoners. If someone was missing, officials alerted every police department and train station within a 25-mile radius and called out the Hitler Youth to search for the escapee.

Even though the castle-converted POW camp was daunting, many prisoners were determined to escape to Switzerland, the closest neutral country. They duplicated keys to various doors, made copies of maps, forged identity papers, manufactured their own tools, and dug tunnels.

Neave learned that a month before his arrival, French lieutenant Alain Le Ray became the first POW at Colditz to achieve a "home run"—a successful escape back to his own country or military unit. Le Ray was on a "park walk," where certain POWs were taken under armed guard to play soccer in a grassy area inside two large wire enclosures below the eastern side of the castle. The men reached the spot by walking along a winding path that went by a deserted terrace house at a sharp bend.

On April 11, 1941, Le Ray, wearing civilian clothes under his uniform and military greatcoat, joined a park walk to attend a POW soccer match. After the game, the guards marched the prisoners up to the path toward the castle entrance. At the sharp bend, when he was momentarily out of sight of the guards behind him, he dashed into the terrace house and hid.

When the group reached the guardhouse at the castle entrance, no one noticed that one of the prisoners was missing. Now in his civilian clothes only, Le Ray emerged from his hiding place, scaled a wall, and ran off. By hiking and stowing away in the back of a truck, he made it to Nuremberg, Germany, about 180 miles away. Having run out of money, he mugged a man in the street, stealing his wallet and overcoat.

Le Ray took a train to Singen, which was only a few miles from the Swiss border. Because it was night, he planned to walk the rest of the way, but a German patrol spotted him. Outrunning the soldiers, he eluded capture by climbing a tree. After he came down, he waited for a train to stop at a nearby station. Counting on the glare of the engine's headlights to prevent anyone from seeing him, he crept up from the side. He gripped on to the front of the engine and rode the train across the border and into Switzerland for the home run. Over the next three months, two other Frenchmen successfully escaped under similar circumstances.

But almost all other attempts ended in capture.

Despite others' setbacks, Neave plotted an escape attempt of his own and made his pitch to the escape committee, a team of prisoners charged with coordinating the various escape attempts so one group wouldn't ruin it for the others.

"I'm going to impersonate a German *Gefreiter* [corporal]," Neave told Captain Patrick Reid, a British POW who headed the committee. "A Polish tailor will alter a shirt, a pair of RAF [Britain's Royal Air Force] trousers, and a ski cap so they look like they are part of a German uniform. They will be dyed green by using paint from the camp theater. I bartered with a Polish orderly for some jackboots. A British officer will carve me a bayonet and scabbard out of wood, which will be hung from a cardboard leather belt with a tinfoil buckle.

"When it's time, I'll line up at evening *appell* wearing my homemade German corporal's uniform under my greatcoat. I'll keep the cap in my pocket. Once the order to dismiss is given, I'll put on my hat while the man behind me pulls off my greatcoat and walks away. I'll march toward the sentry at the gate."

Any person, whether a worker, staff member, or guard, needed to show a brass identity disk to enter or leave the castle. "One of the painters who works in the castle has agreed to give me his disk for money," Neave said.

"What's your plan once you clear the gate?" Reid asked.

"I'll steal one of the bikes in the rack, ride to the station, and catch a train heading for the Swiss frontier. I know it's four hundred miles away, but I have money. I also have a small compass and a map that will be sewn in the liner of my uniform. In addition, a Dutch officer has offered to forge identity papers so I can pass as a foreign worker in Germany."

"How are you going to communicate with the Germans?"

"I can speak their language," Neave replied. "I used to visit this country when I was a teenager so I have a fairly decent command of German. My accent should blend in well with all the foreign workers here in the country who speak different levels of German."

"It seems like you've thought this through," said Reid. "You have to do this at twilight when the light is poor so the guard at the gate won't notice that your uniform is fake. If it gets too dark, the security lights will shine on your painted uniform."

The escape committee gave Neave the okay to try. Everything went according to plan, including obtaining disk number 26 from the bribed painter. On the evening of August 28, Neave put on his greatcoat over the *Gefreiter* clothes and stood at *appell*. As soon as the POWs were dismissed from the inner courtyard, Neave shed the greatcoat and joined several German *Gefreiters*—some of whom weren't armed—and strolled toward the entrance.

The sergeant on duty at the gate collected the numbered brass security disks from the guards as they passed him on their way to their barracks. When it was Neave's turn, he handed in the disk and went left instead of right as the others did.

Suspicious, the sergeant demanded, "Where are you going?"

"I have a message for the commandant from the duty officer," Neave replied in German.

"I don't recognize you," the sergeant said. Then, looking at the disk, he shouted, "Wait! Number twenty-six was reported stolen. Halt!"

Neave cringed and kept on walking, pretending he hadn't heard the sergeant. Just then the arc lights came on, turning his uniform a shiny green, which looked nothing like the German field gray. Alerted by the sergeant's shouts, other guards ran toward Neave, who sprinted for the bike rack. But before he reached it, he heard the sergeant shout, "Halt or I'll shoot!"

Neave stopped, slumped his shoulders, and bowed his head in defeat. When he looked up, he was surrounded by guards whose rifles were pointed at him. *I almost made it,* he thought.

They marched him to a special prison cell where guards discovered his compass, money, and fake ID papers during a thorough search. The next morning, a guard brought him a cup of awful-tasting coffee along with unsettling news: "It's bad that you tried to escape, but pretending to be a German soldier, that is a much more serious offense. You will be court-martialed, found guilty, and then executed by firing squad."

Well, at least I tried, Neave thought. *Death with honor.*

About 10:00 a.m., the guard brought Neave, who was still in his fake uniform, to the commandant's quarters and ordered him to stand in the middle of the room. For the next several hours, German officers in the camp and police from the town arrived in a steady stream to humiliate him. They laughed at him, cursed him, and made him make Nazi salutes. Some of them even goose-stepped around him while shouting, *"Heil Hitler!"*

Neave was stripped of the fake uniform, which was then given to an orderly to put in the commandant's "escape museum"—a room that displayed various clothing, items, and tools used by escapees.

At the evening *appell,* the commandant announced to the assembled POWs, "You won't see *Gefreiter* Neave for a while. He has been posted to the Russian front." Then he chuckled.

The only bright spot in Neave's failed attempt was that he wasn't executed or sent to the Russian front. Instead, he served two weeks in solitary confinement in the town jail and returned to regular prison life.

Although he was extremely disappointed, he was not deterred. While in solitary, he was planning his next escape attempt.

He soon formed a friendship with 24-year-old Dutch officer Anthony "Tony" Luteyn, a lieutenant in the Royal Netherlands East Indies Army. When the war began, Luteyn, who lived in what is now Indonesia, and his fellow Dutch officers there went to the Netherlands to fight for their motherland. But the country soon surrendered. The victorious German High Command offered each Dutch officer a chance to remain free in the Netherlands if he signed a document giving his honor not to harm Nazi interests. While most of the officers from the Netherlands signed, those, like Luteyn, who were from the Dutch colonies, refused because they believed the document asked them to go against their oaths as officers. So Luteyn and his comrades were transported to a POW camp in Germany. Speaking in fluent German, the Dutch prisoners loved to harass the guards and often ignored orders. The Nazis despised them and sent the most stubborn ones—including Luteyn—to Colditz.

Neave and Luteyn agreed to try to escape together to Switzerland by posing as German officers. "We need better-looking uniforms," Neave said.

"The Dutch overcoats are the same shade of field gray as the Germans'," Luteyn said. "With a few alterations from one of our tailors, those coats could be turned into realistic-looking German uniforms."

Meanwhile, Reid, an engineer in his civilian life, discovered that the prisoners' wooden theater stage was built over a guardhouse, which extended outside the POWs' courtyard. He removed several steps from the stage and crawled into a space that was underneath the floor of the stage and above the ceiling of the attic of the guardhouse. Reid figured if he built a trapdoor in the ceiling, escapees could access the guardhouse attic and then its stairway to the lightly guarded back courtyard.

Within weeks, all the preparations were made. On the evening of January 5, 1942, Neave and Luteyn each put on three layers of clothes—first, civilian clothes, then fake German uniforms, and next their own military uniforms for the outer layer.

After the POWs attended *appell,* Reid led the pair to the stage stairs and lifted up two of the steps. The men crawled inside to the space under the stage and above the guard-house. They took off their own uniforms, revealing their fake German ones. Reid opened the trapdoor and helped the men ease into the guardhouse attic below. "Wait ten minutes before you go any farther," he told them. "I need to cover your tracks so the Germans won't know how you escaped. Others will want to sneak out this way, too. Remember, when you see any soldiers, act like you own the place. Good luck."

Neave remained still, although he could barely contain himself because he was yearning to escape. When all was quiet, he and Luteyn brushed the attic dust and dirt off their uniforms. Luteyn turned to Neave and said, *"Bereit? Lass uns gehen."* ("Ready? Let's go.") They walked from the attic down the stairs and into the guardhouse. Several guards sprang to attention when the two passed them. Outside, a sentry saluted them.

The two escapees headed to the back courtyard. In the shadow between two arc lights, they climbed a wall and dropped down on the other side into a park, where they ditched their fake German uniforms. Strolling through town as "civilians," they walked four miles to Leisnig, where they caught the 5:45 a.m. train to Leipzig. Neave wanted to follow the same route that he had tried to take during his escape attempt from Thorn.

While waiting in Leipzig for the next train, which wasn't scheduled to leave for 12 hours, he and Luteyn killed time by going to the movie theater twice. Eventually, they made it to Ulm, Germany, where on the morning of January 7, they tried to buy tickets for their final leg to Engen, a town near the Swiss border. But the ticket seller became suspicious of the pair and called over the local police.

Neave and Luteyn showed the officers forged papers indicating that the two were Dutchmen working with the local *Reichsarbeitsdienst,* an official state labor service. "Yes, your papers seem to be in order," said one of the officers. "But you cannot travel beyond Ulm without getting passes from the local *Reichsarbeitsdienst*. Come, follow me and I will escort you to their office."

Our cover will be blown, Neave thought. *We have to do something.*

When they reached the building, the officer, who was overweight and out of shape, told them, "The office is upstairs. You both speak such good German that I don't need to accompany you. I will wait for you down here."

When they went upstairs, Luteyn whispered to Neave, "What are we going to do? We can't go into the office."

Neave stared at the other end of the hallway. "We're in luck," he said. "There's another stairwell. Let's take it and make a run for it."

They successfully made their getaway, but they were still about 90 miles from the Swiss border. After hiking 25 miles in the snow and bitter cold, they rode a local train and arrived in Singen at about 4:00 a.m. on January 8. Switzerland was so close. While walking on the road, the pair unexpectedly encountered four workmen on bicycles who demanded to know what they were doing at such an early hour. "We're workers for the *Reichsarbeitsdienst*," Luteyn told them.

As the workmen pedaled away, one of the cyclists whispered to the others, "I don't believe them. Let's inform the police."

Overhearing them, Neave told Luteyn, "That's bad. I had

hoped we would cross over the border while it was still dark, but now we'll have to hide for the whole day because the police will be looking for us."

"I noticed a shed about a few hundred yards back," Luteyn said. "Let's stay there until the end of the day."

"I hate to wait when we're so close, but it will be nice to get out of this awful weather."

They went inside the shed—an unlocked garden shack—where they sat on the dirt floor and tried to stay warm. Besides being cold, they were weary and hungry, surviving only on small bites of chocolate and sucking snowballs for drinking water. They soon fell asleep. When they woke up late in the afternoon, they discovered the temperature had dropped so much that their shoes were frozen to the ground.

At 6:00 p.m., they put on long white coats that they found in the hut and walked out, with one carrying a spade and the other an ax so they would look like local workers. Then, tromping in the snow, they made their final push for freedom.

About a mile from the border, they were stopped by a Hitler Youth patrol. "We're from Westphalia [a region in western Germany], sent here by the *Reichsarbeitsdienst*," Luteyn told them.

The head of the patrol seemed satisfied by the answer. "We're on the lookout for two escaped prisoners of war who we suspect are in the area," said the youth leader. "If you see them, tell the police."

"Oh, we will," Neave replied with a straight face.

Around midnight, he and Luteyn neared a border post where German police were stopping cars and checking for the proper documents. On the opposite side, there were no Swiss border agents on duty. The escapees moved a few hundred yards from the post to a clearing that spread to the edge of a forest, which was across a road.

"If we make it to the woods, we're in Switzerland," Neave said, studying his hand-drawn map. "We're so close to freedom. If you're like me, you're wiped out and cold, and your feet hurt from blisters. This will be our final run—one way or the other. Now is the time to run as fast as you can. Good luck, Tony."

"Good luck, Airey. I'll see you in Switzerland."

They dropped their tools and shook hands. Then they bolted for the border, hoping no one would see them. Because the snow had covered many rocks, roots, and holes, they stumbled and fell repeatedly in their mad scramble to reach the woods. Despite their stumbles, they made it safely.

Breathing heavily while leaning against a tree, Neave looked up at Luteyn and said, "Welcome to Switzerland."

Airey Neave was the first British officer to escape from Colditz and make it back to the United Kingdom. After receiving the Military Cross (the country's third highest military medal), he was promoted to captain. He was then recruited by MI-9, a department in the country's military intelligence

agency responsible for helping resistance fighters and Allied POWs. Given the code name "Saturday," Neave set up escape routes throughout northern Europe for downed pilots and POW escapees.

After the war, he served with the International Military Tribunal at the Nuremberg Trials, where Nazis were prosecuted for war crimes and crimes against humanity. Neave later was elected to the British Parliament and served many years until he was assassinated in 1979 in a car bomb attack carried out by the Irish National Liberation Army. He was 63.

Following his escape, Tony Luteyn rejoined the Dutch East Indies Army in a unit based in Australia. For his actions, he earned the Bronze Cross. He eventually settled in The Hague, Netherlands, where he changed the spelling of his name to Luteijn. He died in 2003 at the age of 85.

According to Henry Chancellor, author of Colditz: The Definitive History, 32 POWs successfully escaped from Colditz: 12 French, 11 British, 7 Dutch, 1 Belgian, and 1 Pole.

After the war, the town of Colditz became a part of Soviet-controlled East Germany. The Russians converted the castle into a prison camp for political prisoners. It later became a home for the aged, a nursing facility, a hospital, and a psychiatric clinic. After 1996, the castle was renovated and turned into a museum.

THE WOODEN WARHORSE

Flight Lieutenant Oliver Philpot

No. 42 Squadron, Coastal Command, Royal Air Force

As a member of the escape committee, Flight Lieutenant Oliver Philpot had heard some outlandish ideas from fellow POWs about how to break out of Stalag Luft III. But the one that Lieutenants Eric Williams and Richard "Mike" Codner presented was by far the craziest.

"And yet," he told them, "it just might work."

Opened in the spring of 1942 near Sagan (now Żagań), Poland, the German-run POW camp eventually covered 60 acres and held more than 10,000 aviators, including 7,500 Americans and 2,500 members of Britain's Royal Air Force (RAF). The complex was designed to prevent prisoners from tunneling to freedom. The barracks were built far from the perimeter fences to discourage POWs from digging a tunnel because it would require an extremely long one. The buildings also sat aboveground so guards could see anyone digging underneath them. Excavated subsoil was sandy and yellow and easily noticeable on the clothes of diggers or on the gray topsoil when spread on the ground. To further foil any escape attempts, the Germans buried seismographic microphones around the guarded, double-fenced perimeter to pick up sounds of any digging.

Despite all the reasons why tunneling their way out seemed futile, prisoners tried anyway. During Stalag Luft III's first year, POWs started 40 tunnels . . . and not one led to a single escape because the Germans discovered them all in various stages of construction.

So when Williams and Codner told Philpot, who was the escape coordinator for their barracks, their plan for a tunnel, he had his doubts. But it was so clever—ingenious, really—he took the scheme to the escape committee.

"It's quite simple," Philpot explained. "We build a vaulting horse like the ones we used to have in our school gyms. It will be about three feet high and two feet wide at the base, hollow inside with solid sides made from the wooden boxes that the Red Cross sends us. We hide a man inside the horse and carry it from the canteen [the prison social club] to a spot about a hundred feet from the fence. He digs while prisoners on top are vaulting over the horse for exercise, making noise to drown out the buried microphones. At the end of each digging session, he climbs out of the tunnel with bags of sand that he attaches to the inside of the horse. He covers up the hole with boards and topsoil and then he and the full bags are carried back. Every day, we return to the same spot with a digger inside the horse, and he continues his work while others exercise." Philpot added that once the tunnel is completed, the escapees would try to make their way by train and boat to Sweden, a neutral country in the war, about 500 miles away.

The committee gave its approval, which meant it would oversee all stages of the escape attempt. It would provide the escapees with the items they would need after their breakout—forged papers, money, passports, clothing, food, equipment, train schedules, and maps.

The vaulting horse scheme excited Philpot even though he wasn't originally invited to escape. The 28-year-old Canadian-born veteran pilot assumed he would sit out the remainder of the war as a POW ever since his capture one and a half years earlier. On December 11, 1941, he was flying a British torpedo bomber for the RAF off the coast of Norway when he and his crew attacked a German convoy. During the assault, antiaircraft fire crippled his plane, forcing him to ditch in the North Sea. Before the plane sank, he and his three crew members climbed into a raft and floated for two days before sailors in a passing German naval vessel nabbed them.

Williams, 32, was a navigator aboard a British bomber when it was shot down during a raid over Germany on December 18, 1942. He eluded the enemy for three days before he was caught. Taken to a POW camp near Schubin (now Szubin), Poland, he met Codner, 21, of the Royal Artillery, who four days earlier was captured in Tunisia in North Africa. Forming a fast friendship, the two broke out of the prison together through a tunnel but were apprehended and then sent to Stalag Luft III. Undeterred, they were now plotting their next escape.

After getting the consent from the German commandant, the prisoners built the vaulting horse. But digging didn't start right away. For the first week, they used the horse for vaulting only. Occasionally, someone would act like a klutz and deliberately knock it over so the guards, who were called goons by the POWs, could see there was nothing hidden inside. Suspicious as always, the guards inspected the horse inside and out anyway, but found nothing. Once the Germans became used to seeing the horse carried from the canteen out to the compound and back, they ignored it.

The scheme reminded Philpot of the Trojan horse in Greek mythology. In the story, the Greek army built a large wooden horse that hid 30 soldiers and left it outside their enemy's port city of Troy. After the Greek army sailed away, the Trojans pulled the horse into their walled-in city as a victory trophy. That night the Greek soldiers emerged from the horse and opened Troy's gates for the rest of the Greek army, which had sailed back. The Greek forces destroyed Troy, ending a 10-year siege.

On July 8, 1943, the digging began under the vaulting horse. At first, Williams and Codner did all the work because they were the only ones attempting to escape. Using a stolen trowel and tools made out of tin cans, they took turns hollowing out a 5-foot-deep, 2½-foot-wide vertical shaft, which they shored up with wood from boxes and stolen bricks.

Then they started burrowing the tunnel. They propped up the first seven feet of the roof and sides with bed boards because that section was directly below the landing area of the vaulters. Without sufficient reinforcement, the men's jumping would likely cause a cave-in.

At the end of each day, the digger hauled up a dozen bags of subsoil and closed the shaft with bed boards placed horizontally 18 inches below the surface. He placed two small three-pound bags of sand on top of the boards to prevent them from wobbling. Over the bags and boards, the digger replaced the original topsoil that he had removed under the horse before going into the shaft. The digger also smoothed out the soil to eliminate any footprints he made under the horse. That way, if a guard walked over the shaft after the horse was carried away, he wouldn't notice any difference with the rest of the ground or that there were footprints where there shouldn't be any.

When the men returned the horse to the canteen, the digger, who was all but naked because it was so hot in the tunnel, crawled out. He hustled into a small room, where he cleaned up, got dressed, and swept away any telltale yellow subsoil on the floor. The digging tools, hooks, and bags were taken to the adjoining barbershop, where they were hidden under removable floorboards that were otherwise held in place by specially made nails. The bags of yellow subsoil were emptied on the roof, where the sun turned the dirt gray, matching the topsoil.

One day, Codner was working in the tunnel when a section of the roof gave way, burying him and causing a small hole to form on the surface. Before guards spotted it, a quick-thinking vaulter deliberately tripped and fell over the hole, covering it with his body, and then lay there pretending he was injured. Meanwhile, down below, Codner frantically dug his way free of the collapse. Using planks taken from the shaft, he shored up the cave-in.

After spending several hours a day for two months in the cramped 2½-foot-by-2½-foot tunnel, Williams and Codner had burrowed 40 feet toward the fence. They were exhausted and asked Philpot to help dig and join in the escape. "Sure, but on two conditions," Philpot said. "First, it stays a three-man scheme. No one else. And, second, when I escape from the tunnel, I go my own way."

The next day at the canteen, Philpot undressed, leaving on his T-shirt and shorts, and crawled under the horse. With the nearest guard about 50 yards away, the men carried the vaulting horse to the correct spot and set it down. Philpot jumped to the ground and hung bits of sackcloth on tiny nails to prevent sharp-eyed guards from seeing any movement between the tiny gaps of wood in the sides of the horse.

On his knees, Philpot felt around until he found the top of the shaft. He scooped up the surface dirt and put it in a pink bag. Next, he removed the stabilizing bags and pried up the boards. *There's the shaft*, he thought. *It's smaller than I thought*. He stifled a sneeze when the tunnel's dank, earthy smell reached his nostrils.

He slipped into the shaft and, at the bottom, scrunched his body until he could fit into the tunnel. With his hands in front of him, he squirmed forward on his belly into the blackness. The air was thick and stale. There were no air vents, no breathing tubes. He kept wriggling onward like a worm, trying not to think about cave-ins or suffocation or getting caught. *How much farther?*

Then from overhead he heard thumping that grew louder for several seconds before fading. *Must be the boys above doing their daily run around the compound*. He continued inching headfirst until his knuckles hit the end. *Finally*.

With the trowel, he began scraping away at the wall in front of him and then pushing the loose dirt behind him with his right arm, much like a turtle uses its flippers on the beach. The longer he dug, the more uneasy he felt. Sweat had drenched his entire body. The isolation, blackness, and confinement preyed on his mind. A terrifying sensation crept over him—the feeling of being buried alive. *I can't stand this. I need light. I need air. I need to sit up.*

Because he had no room to turn around, he had to back up feetfirst, pushing the yellow subsoil until he came to the base of the shaft. Even though the vault horse above him had blocked out the sun, there was enough light filtering through the cracks and crevices of the horse to assure him that he was safe for the moment. The slits of light were most welcoming and so were the sounds of his comrades vaulting above him.

"Hello?" he called up.

"Okay down there?" asked Williams, who was pretending to talk to one of the vaulters in case a guard was watching him.

"Yes, Eric," replied Philpot, whose anxiety was slowly draining away. Gathering his courage, he went back into the cramped tunnel and continued to dig. While pushing his second load of subsoil, some dirt from the sides of the tunnel closed in on him, almost forming a seal around his head, neck, and chest. He began to panic, flailing frantically to free himself from the mucky grip.

His heart racing and his nerves charged by terror, he squirmed, kicked, and thrashed his way to the shaft. Panting and gulping in the clammy air, he made up his mind that this was all a terrible mistake. *I shouldn't be doing this*, he thought. *I'll tell Williams and Codner to get someone else. I can't stay in this tunnel any longer. Yes, I've lost my nerve, but I can retrieve my honor by working on a normal tunnel, one with shoring and lights and space to move about.*

Hearing the vaulting POWs above him, Philpot calmed down. After filling all 12 bags, he put them on hooks on the inside of the horse. He replaced the boards over the shaft, covered them with the gray topsoil, and then called out to Williams, "Ready to go in, Eric."

The vaulters hauled the horse, with Philpot inside it, back to the canteen. After Philpot cleaned up, Williams asked, "So, Ollie, how was it down there?"

"It's no fun and a tight squeeze, but I can manage," Philpot replied. The words that came out of his mouth surprised him. As much as he hated working in the tunnel, he wasn't ready to quit. Instead of fretting over the tight and dangerous conditions, he channeled his thoughts and actions toward one goal: escape.

But breathing in all that dust, dirt, and sand, and toiling strenuously in a chamber with little air, made the trio sick. Williams ended up in the sick bay hut for a week with lung problems.

To pick up the pace and lessen the difficulty of tunneling, two began working at the same time. After both were carried out in the vaulting horse, one dug in the tunnel while the other stayed in the shaft. The digger pushed the dirt onto a piece of canvas, which was attached to a rope. Once it was full, the man in the shaft pulled it toward himself and scooped it into bags. This way, they were able to fill 36 bags a day instead of 12.

But because it was impossible to carry out all 36 bags and two men at once, they left the bags in the shaft, sealed it up, and returned to the canteen empty-handed. Later in the evening, the prisoners brought out the horse again for another vaulting session. This time, one of the members of the three-man escape team retrieved 12 bags. The same was true the next afternoon and evening. Then the cycle was repeated: fill 36 bags, then take out 12 one day and 24 the next.

After three months, Williams emerged from a digging

session and told the others, "I struck a large, strong upright post down there. It's obviously one of the posts of the inner fence."

"We're getting close," said Codner. "The outer fence is about ten feet away."

"It's time we fine-tune our plans for when we break out of here," said Philpot.

Because Codner could speak French, he and Williams were going to impersonate French workers—Marcel Levasseur and Michel Conde, respectively. They planned to travel together on trains to the north coast of Poland, hop on a ship to German-occupied Denmark, and then, with the help of the resistance movement, reach Sweden. The escape committee advised Williams, who spoke only English, to play dumb or at least say, *"Ich bin Ausländer, nicht verstehen."* ("I am a foreigner. I don't understand.")

Philpot's plan was to take the train from Sagan to the port city of Danzig (now Gdańsk), Poland, where he would stow away aboard a Sweden-bound ship. He took on the identity of a made-up person—Norwegian Jon Jorgensen, a margarine salesman, which was Philpot's actual prewar civilian job. But even though two Norwegian POWs offered to teach him some basic Norwegian, he stopped after three lessons, claiming he couldn't learn the language in a few weeks. "If I meet a real Norwegian, I'm sunk," Philpot told the others. "The solution is not to meet a real Norwegian."

To travel anywhere in German-occupied territory, the escapees needed passports, letters, certificates, passes, identification cards, and permits. POWs skilled in forgery and with access to prison offices were busy creating the fake documents for the trio.

One prisoner made a compass for Philpot. The casing was molded from a four-inch-wide piece of a phonograph record. Sticking up from the center of the casing was a record player needle that held a circular card with various directional degrees written on them. Pasted underneath the card were two pieces of a razor blade that had been magnetized by the camp electric light circuit. The card markings were written with glowing phosphorous, which had been added from the faces of broken watches so he could see them in the dark. Covering the contents was a piece of glass.

Because POWs wore their military uniforms, the escapees needed civilian clothes. Using bedsheets, blankets, curtains, and old uniforms, prisoners who were tailors created apparel that fit the identities of the fake persons.

Williams and Codner were given clothes that French workers would wear. For Philpot, the tailors made a double-breasted sport coat with elbow patches. "It's been used in two other unsuccessful escapes," a POW told Philpot. "Here's hoping the third time is the charm." His civilian pants were altered from a pilot's dress uniform. Shirts were made of wool. An RAF officer's black tie was transformed by stitching a white design on it. To complete the image of a businessman, Philpot was given a pair of dress shoes, a small attaché case, and a homburg (a stiff, felt, black, semi-formal hat).

After more than 100 days of digging, the tunnel was nearly completed, so the trio decided to escape on the night of October 29 when the moon was dark. Because all three couldn't fit in the horse at the same time, Codner volunteered to go into the tunnel during the afternoon vaulting exercises and remain there while the other two would join him in the evening session.

On the morning of escape day, Philpot shaved the ends of his mustache so it matched the one worn by Nazi dictator Adolf Hitler. "Very goon-like, Ollie, very goon-like," a prisoner told Philpot. "But it looks jolly fine."

In the afternoon, the POWs took the horse out. In it were Codner and Philpot, parcels of supplies for all three, and tools to dig out the exit hole. While Codner worked at the end of the tunnel, Philpot placed the parcels in cavities that he had carved out in the dirt. When it was time for him to temporarily leave the tunnel, he told Codner, "We're going to make it, aren't we, Mike."

"You bet," Codner replied.

As Philpot climbed into the horse and began closing up the shaft, he felt like a gravedigger who had just covered the coffin of a friend. He shuddered at the thought of what Codner was going through—completely sealed underground, where he would remain for several hours. Philpot got the chills thinking about it.

Later that afternoon, the guards did a roll call. To cover for the missing Codner, one of the RAF officers pretended to be ill and went to sick bay, where he was counted first.

Then he jumped out of bed and, without the Germans noticing, made it to the formation, where he was counted again.

Philpot was dressed in his businessman's attire, which
was under a long Polish army coat buttoned up to his neck
to hide his nice collared shirt and suit and tie. Fortunately,
it was cold outside, so wearing the coat didn't raise any
suspicion.

He met up with Williams in the music room of the canteen, where an unusually large number of fellow prisoners
had gathered to say good-bye to the pair: "Good luck, Ollie."
"Hope you make it." "I don't want to see you back here again."
Comrades shook Philpot's hand and patted him on the back.

"It's all very nice of them, Eric, but won't the goons get
suspicious seeing so many prisoners in here?" he asked.

"We'll find out real soon," said Williams. "One of them
is heading this way." It was the commander of the guards,
who, thanks to his suspicious nature, had a talent for discovering tunnels before they were completed. Members of
the prison church choir were there, so Williams told them,
"Start singing. Everyone, join in."

Grabbing sheet music from the choir, men who had never
gone to church services began singing, "For he shall give his
angels charge over thee . . ." They stopped when the commander entered the room. "Go on," he told them. "Don't let
me stop you." When they finished the song, he smiled and left
the canteen, unaware of the true purpose of the gathering.

It was now the moment for Philpot and Codner to get
into the horse, which, for the first time, would include a third

man—a New Zealander who was the smallest POW in camp. His job would be to close up the shaft after the pair entered the tunnel. As prisoners carried out the horse, they acted as if it wasn't any heavier than normal even though it was.

After they set it down, Williams opened the shaft, jumped in it, and checked on Codner, who responded, "I'm doing fine and ready to get out of here."

While the vaulters exercised and made noise, Philpot lowered himself into the shaft. Then, after wishing them good luck, the New Zealander covered up the shaft. *There's no going back now*, Philpot thought. The escape from Stalag Luft III had begun.

Codner was still digging at the head of the tunnel, trying to break through to the surface while Williams shoved the loose dirt back to Philpot. Not having worked in the tunnel with all their clothes on before, the men were drenched in sweat even though they had taken off their overcoats. In the hot, stifling, and smelly air, Philpot fought the urge to rip off his clothes.

To hide their fair skin and help avoid detection from searchlights once they climbed out of the tunnel, they took extra precautions. They each put on over their clothes a Red Cross vest and long underwear, both dyed black, and an extra pair of large dark socks over their polished shoes. They wrapped dark scarves around their necks and wore gloves.

Philpot felt through his woolen vest for the safety pin fastened to his right-hand jacket pocket, which held all his important papers and money. It was secure.

Soon he detected a whiff of cool, fresh air coming from the tunnel head. "Mike just broke through," Williams said. "Will you tie my kit bag to my foot?"

Philpot retrieved the kit bag from the wall cavity and tied it around Williams's ankle. Then he grabbed his own two parcels, including his attaché case, which contained the homburg among other things. The parcels were wrapped in Red Cross underclothing dyed black.

When Codner finished widening the opening of the exit, Williams reached back in the darkness and groped around until he grasped Philpot's hand. "Good luck, Ollie."

"Good luck, Eric."

After all those months of hard work, planning, and coordinating, the moment that the trio had dreamed about was here. No one said a word.

In an instant, Philpot found himself alone. His fellow escapees had vanished. He crawled to the exit shaft and looked up. Stars twinkled as if beckoning him to emerge. Remaining still, he waited to hear gunfire and shouts from guards. There was only silence. *Oh, good*, he thought. *Mike and Eric made it to the woods without anyone seeing them. Now it's my turn.*

He poked his head out of the opening. Beams from the permanently fixed arc lights high on telephone poles lit up the perimeter. He glanced at the nearest watchtower about 70 feet away. The sentry was peering into the camp.

Philpot ducked when a swinging searchlight from another watchtower swept over the exit hole. He froze, wondering if an alert sentry would notice. *Still silence. Good. Well, waiting any longer is useless.* He lifted his parcel and attaché case through the hole and placed them on the surface. Without any further reconnaissance, he scrambled out of the tunnel. Picking up his possessions, he streaked across the open area and into the woods. He plowed through low scrub brush until he forced himself to pull up and listen. *I don't hear anything. So far, so good.*

Fifteen minutes later, "Jon Jorgensen" was standing in the ticket line at the Sagan train station, which bustled with civilians and military men. A few seconds had elapsed before he realized that the young Frenchman in front of him in the black beret and brown mackintosh was Codner. Philpot didn't let him know who was behind him in case someone was watching them. *I can never be too careful,* he thought. *Besides, we're taking different trains.*

After Philpot boarded the train, a plainclothes policeman demanded to see his passport. While studying it, the officer snapped, "Your photo is not stamped as it should have been when you entered the country."

Oh, no. The forgers forgot to stamp it. Now what? "Well, sir, I wouldn't know anything about that. I hope that's not a problem." The officer eyed Philpot's unconcerned manner and then handed the passport back and moved on.

Philpot gazed at the photo and smiled. It was that of an RAF pilot who didn't look anything like him. The picture was of a man with a round face and a handlebar mustache. *Maybe it was a good thing the forgers didn't stamp it,* Philpot thought. *The police officer was so intent on the missing stamp that he didn't even notice how different the photo was from my appearance.*

Philpot reached Danzig 24 hours after the escape and spent the next day scouting ships until he saw one flying the Swedish flag. It was the *Aralizz.* That night, while a crane was loading coal onto the vessel, he entered the dock unnoticed. Because a sentry was guarding the gangway, Philpot climbed one of the ship's stern cables.

Tired and anxious from the events of the last 48 hours, he found his ascent harder than he'd imagined. His muscles burned, and he was running out of steam. *I'm so close, so close. I can't give up.* His arms and hands were shaking from the strain, but he mustered just enough strength to get up and over the gunwale and onto the deck. *I made it!*

He sprawled on the deck to catch his breath. As he lay in a pool of his own sweat, he listened for the sounds of a search—running and shouting and dogs barking. But all he heard was the clanking and rattling of the crane and the rumble of coal tumbling into the ship. *Great, no one saw me!*

He needed a place to hide on the ship. As a matter of routine, the Germans, often accompanied by dogs, searched all ships from bow to stern. They were so strict that Nazi patrol boats often intercepted vessels two or three hours after leaving port.

I'll make myself known to the crew, he decided. *I have to take the chance they'll hide me from the Germans.* Philpot entered the galley, where hot chocolate was simmering on the stove. He couldn't resist. Using a large ladle as a cup, he took several swigs of the sweet drink. *I haven't tasted any-thing this good in nearly two years.*

Going to the nearest cabin, he knocked and entered, startling a steward. "Shh," Philpot said. "It's all right. I'm a Canadian flier who has escaped a POW camp."

"No," said the steward, who appeared visibly afraid. "I can do nothing. You must leave the ship immediately, or you will get us all in trouble."

Soon they were joined by two sailors and the captain, who demanded that Philpot leave. "I can't," the escapee declared. "I won't. I've come too far. Let me hide in the coal bunker. No one will find me there."

While the captain discussed the situation with his first mate, another sailor led Philpot to the coal bunker and hid him there for nine hours. Then the sailor moved Philpot to an empty storage tank, where the escapee remained during the German inspection. The tank was oily and as dark as the tunnel, with barely enough air to breathe. But he didn't care. He felt safe. Soon he heard the engines coughing and felt their vibration and the slight swaying of the ship. The *Aralizz* had cast off. He wanted to yell in triumph, "Magnificent! Well done! You did it!" Instead, he silently mouthed the words, just to be on the safe side.

The ship docked in Stockholm on November 4. Philpot was taken to the British consulate, where he was welcomed and congratulated as the first POW to escape from Stalag Luft III. While waiting to get processed and before his flight to England, he wandered the city and bought new clothes, including a Nordic-style suit.

Ten days after his arrival, he received a phone call from the British attaché, who said, "You might want to come down to the consulate right now. A couple of friends of yours wish to see you."

When Philpot entered the office, the attaché pointed to the corner of the room behind the escapee and said, "I think you've met these lads before."

Philpot turned around. There, getting up from their chairs, were Williams and Codner.

Pointing to Philpot, Codner shook his head in a disapproving way and said, "Where'd you get that awful-looking suit?" They all burst out laughing and then embraced.

"Gee," said Philpot, "at such an astounding moment as this, you would've thought that at least one of us would've said something more dramatic than, 'Where'd you get that awful-looking suit.'"

After escaping from the prison camp, Eric Williams and Mike Codner had traveled by train to the Polish port city of Stettin (now Szczecin), where they made contact with French dockworkers who were members of the resistance. With the underground's help, the two men were smuggled aboard a ship bound for Copenhagen, Denmark.

Before it could sail, German officers came aboard with

sniffer dogs to search the vessel. The captain, who wanted to help the escapees, plied the Germans with schnapps to distract them from their work and secretly peppered the dogs' noses to successfully prevent them from smelling his human cargo hidden in the chain locker of the ship's bilge.

After docking in Nazi-occupied Denmark, Williams and Codner waited several days until it was safe to sneak out of the country. A small fishing boat operated by a resistance fighter took them to Sweden, where they contacted the British consulate and reunited with Philpot.

Williams, who received the Military Cross for his escape, returned to flying, but in the Philippines, where he served alongside Americans. His wife was killed in Liverpool, England, during a German bombing run, and two of his brothers were killed in action while serving overseas. After the war, he settled in England and wrote several books about POWs, including his own experiences. One of his books, The Wooden Horse, was turned into a movie of the same name in 1950. He spent much of his later years living on his sailboat, Escaper, while touring the Mediterranean with his second wife, Sibyl. He died in 1983 at the age of 72.

Codner, who was awarded the Military Cross, remained with the Royal Artillery until the end of the war. He then moved to Malaysia, where he died in 1952 at the age of 31.

After his escape, Oliver Philpot, who was awarded the Distinguished Flying Cross and the Military Cross, served in England as a senior scientific officer for the Air Ministry. Then he resumed his career in the food industry in the United

Kingdom, becoming chief executive officer of Findus, a major frozen food company. He wrote a book about his wartime experiences, Stolen Journey, which was a key source for this story. He later became managing director of Remploy, a British organization that helped disabled people find employment. Philpot died in London in 1993 at the age of 80.

ON A WING AND A PRAYER

Lieutenant Robert "Bob" Hoover

4th Fighter Squadron, 52nd Fighter Group,

US Army Air Forces

German guards shoved Flight Officer Bob Hoover against a cement wall pockmarked with bullet holes. Then they pointed their handguns at his head.

Their captain, who had tried but failed to coax any information out of the American POW other than name, rank, and serial number, angrily slapped his swagger stick against his leg as he stomped toward Hoover. Stopping inches from the pilot's face, the captain hissed, "You have one minute to answer my questions, or you will be shot."

Believing his life was over, Hoover refused to crack and cooperate. He showed no emotion while giving the same response he had uttered so many times since his capture: "Robert A. Hoover, Flight Officer, 20443029."

Infuriated, the captain, speaking in German, ordered

the guards to holster their handguns and pick up their rifles. Switching to English for Hoover's benefit, the captain bellowed, "Ready!" The guards swung their rifles to shoulder height.

As tears began to well in his eyes, Hoover thought, *I don't want to die this way, alone and humiliated, without a chance to defend myself.*

"Aim!" The guards cocked their weapons. Although the terror he felt nearly caused him to buckle to the ground, Hoover was determined not to display any fear. He stared stone-faced at his executioners and waited for what he believed would be the last word he would ever hear in his life: "Fire!"

Growing up in Nashville, Tennessee, Hoover yearned to fly ever since he was five years old and listened to the news on the radio about Charles Lindbergh's historic nonstop solo flight across the Atlantic Ocean in 1927. Ten years later, at age 15, Hoover used the $2 he earned a week bagging groceries to pay for 15-minute flying lessons. After nearly a year, he made his first solo flight.

In 1940, on his eighteenth birthday, he joined the Tennessee Air National Guard. After his squadron was transferred to the US Army Air Forces, he trained as a fighter pilot. By 1943, he was skilled in flying most American and British planes. Considered one of the best pilots in the entire corps in World War II, he was promoted to flight leader in the 4th Fighter Squadron, 52nd Fighter Group based on the French island of Corsica in the Mediterranean Sea.

On February 9, 1944, the tall, lanky 22-year-old hopped into a bomb-carrying Spitfire Mark V and led a four-plane mission to patrol the coastal waters between Cannes, France, and Genoa, Italy. They attacked a German convoy off the coast of Nice, France, but then the Americans encountered four of Germany's most versatile fighter plane, the Focke-Wulf 190.

During the ensuing dogfight, Hoover watched in horror as the plane of his roommate and closest friend, James "Monty" Montgomery, burst into flames and spiraled to its doom. Heartbroken and angry, Hoover zoomed head-on toward an enemy plane and let loose with his .50-caliber machine gun. The German plane erupted in flames and smoke before plunging into the sea. The satisfaction Hoover felt over notching his first kill quickly vanished when two enemy planes began shooting at him.

Firing back, Hoover damaged one of the attacking air-craft. But the other Focke-Wulf 190 came up from underneath him, unleashing a flurry of bullets. Suddenly, he felt searing pain in his buttocks and the back of his thighs. "Ahh, I've been hit!" he radioed. Seconds later, his engine exploded, turning the plane's nose into a ball of flames and smearing the windshield in spewed oil.

Having lost power and unable to see, Hoover knew he couldn't save his plane. Calling for amphibious rescue planes, he radioed, "I'm going down at sea, so alert the Dumbos to start flying."

He then jettisoned the canopy and jumped out. Hoover hit the frigid water hard, knocking the wind out of him and intensifying the pain from his wounds. He tried to inflate his little life raft, but shrapnel from the dogfight had sliced it up. As he freed himself from the parachute harness, he thought, *Stay calm and fall back on your survival training. There's nothing more I can do except float and wait to be rescued. Someone will come along. But who will find me first? The Germans or friendly faces?*

After bobbing in the body-numbing water for four hours about 20 miles off the coast of Nice, Hoover wondered if anyone would rescue him. Darkness had begun to settle in when he heard the sound of a diesel engine. *A ship! Finally! Please be a friendly one.*

He hoped his ordeal was over. But his troubles were only beginning, because the vessel was a German corvette, a small warship that escorted convoys. The sailors tossed him a lifeline. A combatant to the bitter end, Hoover shouted, "No, no! I won't take it. I'd rather stay in the water than go aboard an enemy ship."

The corvette cruised past him and then turned around, coming within a few feet of him. This time, the sailors reached down and pulled him onto the deck. *I can't believe this is happening to me*, he thought. *I'm now a prisoner of war!*

On board, he was strip-searched and then given civilian

clothes to wear while his uniform dried. Although he was treated humanely, Hoover didn't receive any medical care for his wounds, which, although painful, didn't seem too serious. When questioned, the tough airman replied with only his name, rank, and serial number. After the ship docked, guards locked him up in a dark, rat-infested local jail. Never had the pilot felt so despondent and worried, because he didn't know what fate awaited him. He was no longer in control of his life. Slumped on the floor, he thought, *The rats are more free than I am.*

The next day, guards took him to a Cannes hotel, which an enemy battalion had turned into its headquarters. When he refused to answer the German commander's questions, Hoover was strapped to a marble column in the hotel lobby. For the next two days, Nazi sympathizers and relatives of German soldiers marched past the prisoner, cursing him, spitting at him, and slapping him. He could do nothing but take the abuse.

Moved to a barbed-wire-encircled prison in Marseille, France, Hoover focused on one goal: escape. To his surprise, one of the three iron bars in the window of his concrete cell was loose. *This might be my chance,* he thought. He removed a metal support beam from the chair in his cell to use as a chisel. Wrapping the loose bar with his flight jacket to muffle the sound, he used the heel of his shoe to pound on the beam, which chipped away at the cement frame around the window's bars.

After a few hours of work, he loosened all three bars.

Late that night, he removed them, squeezed through the opening, and crawled out onto a ledge, which was ten feet above the ground. *Can I jump that far without the guards hearing me?* he wondered. Tense and anxious, he told himself, *Well, there's no turning back.*

He lowered himself from the ledge and dropped to the frozen ground with a thud, causing the guard dogs to bark in alarm. After sprinting to the prison's barbed wire fence, he started to climb it when searchlights found him—and so did the dogs. They clamped their jaws on his pant legs and yanked him away from the fence. Before they could maul him, the dogs were called off by the guards, who beat Hoover with the butts of their rifles and then tossed him into solitary confinement in a dark, windowless basement cell.

Disheartened that he didn't get away, Hoover thought, *Well, if they don't execute me, I'll try again.*

The next day he was handcuffed and put on a passenger train with two armed soldiers who were assigned to guard only him. By seeing the position of the winter sun, he could tell the train was heading north toward Switzerland, a neutral country. He began plotting his next escape attempt.

After Hoover claimed he needed to use the toilet, one of the guards led him to the tiny one-person bathroom and took off the handcuffs. Once inside, Hoover locked the door, kicked out the window, squeezed through the opening, and leaped from the train.

He landed in a deep snowbank, which was good because it cushioned the impact of his jump. But it was bad because the snow was so thick and heavy that he struggled to move forward. Hoover had taken five steps when German soldiers began shooting at him. Unable to run, he raised his hands in surrender. After he was dragged back onto the train, he was shackled to his seat for the remainder of what turned out to be a 400-mile trip. *I'm zero for two in escape attempts.*

He spent the night in a jail cell in Mulhouse, France, about 20 miles from the Swiss border. Because it was customary for the Germans to punish any soldier whose prisoner escaped (however briefly), Hoover's guard was locked in a cell next to him. Throughout the night, the guard cursed and yelled at Hoover and banged on the cell door's bars to keep him awake.

The next day, the Germans transported Hoover 200 miles to Oberursel, Germany, home of a POW camp for captured Allied pilots. Put in solitary confinement for days for his earlier escape attempts, Hoover received nothing but bread, water, and thin cabbage soup. Two German officers—one nice, the other mean—repeatedly tried to get him to talk at the interrogation center. Even though his untreated wounds were now infected, and he was constantly hungry and feeling weaker, he refused to cooperate in exchange for food and medical treatment.

When he overheard a new American prisoner, who had been a gunner on a B-17 bomber, answering the German officers' questions, Hoover was furious. He lashed out, "Shut up, you coward! You're going to cost fellow airmen their lives!"

Hoover continued to yell at the POW until an irate guard stormed into Hoover's cell, stuck a pistol to his head, and warned, "If you don't keep quiet, I'll blow your head off."

The following day, guards brought Hoover to a dingy room where a German officer offered him a tray of roast beef, boiled potatoes, and steamed vegetables. "You must be terribly hungry," the officer said. "Let's have a conversation while you eat."

The tantalizing aroma tempted the half-starved Hoover. *That looks and smells so good,* he thought. As much as he wanted to devour every morsel, he wouldn't take a bite.

Shuffling through papers in a file, the German said, "We know you were flying a Spitfire." He began asking questions about the plane and the mission. But Hoover remained mum while pushing away the food.

A day later, the Germans tried again to get him to talk, this time with an impatient captain who threatened, "Cooperate or be shot."

By the tone in the captain's voice and evil in his eyes, Hoover believed him. *I mean nothing to the Germans, so why wouldn't they kill me?*

Even if it led to his death, Hoover wasn't going to cave. In a slow, measured voice, he said, "Robert A. Hoover, Flight Officer, 20443029."

Exploding in fury, the captain screamed at Hoover and then bellowed orders in German. Four guards hauled the prisoner out of the building and slammed him up against a wall marred by hundreds of bullet holes. "For your failure to cooperate, you must die," the captain declared.

Hoover didn't twitch or change his expressionless face.

"Ready!" the captain ordered the guards as Hoover stared at the rifle barrels pointed at him. *So this is the last sight I will ever see.*

"Aim!" Before uttering the one word that would end Hoover's life, the German hesitated. He studied Hoover to see if the POW would, at this last possible moment, finally agree to talk.

Resigned to his fate, Hoover locked eyes with his executioners and remained silent. *I hope death will be instant so I won't feel the pain from the bullets.*

One second passed. Then another and another. The mounting tension and crushing fear were almost too much for Hoover to bear. He was on the verge of collapsing.

Unexpectedly, the captain mumbled something to the guards. Then he spun on his heel and stormed back into the building. The guards lowered their weapons. They ushered the resolute but shaken POW back to his cell, where it took a few hours before he regained control of his emotions. Fear soon gave way to a new awareness: *This planned execution was all a ruse, just a ploy to get me to talk.*

Because it didn't work, Hoover felt inspired to attempt another escape. Under his uniform, he had been wearing a turtleneck long-sleeved shirt that the boat captain had given him when he was captured. A few days after the fake execution scheme, Hoover put the shirt over his military shirt so he wouldn't look like a prisoner. After another fruitless grilling at the interrogation center, he was allowed to use the bathroom there. When the guards weren't looking, he quietly emerged and crawled out of the building's exit door. Then, acting like a civilian worker, he walked toward the main gate without drawing any attention.

But at the gate, a guard started talking to him. Not understanding German, Hoover kept moving until the guard grabbed him by the shoulder and began shouting. Hearing the commotion, another guard came over and recognized the prisoner. At gunpoint, the German ordered Hoover back to his cell and then pistol-whipped his head, causing scars that would last a lifetime.

The next day Hoover was stuffed in one of several boxcars packed with POWs on a train that took them to Stalag Luft I prison camp located on a peninsula that jutted out into the Baltic Sea on Germany's northern coast near the city of Barth. The camp, which held more than 1,000 Allied airmen, was surrounded by double ten-foot-tall barbed wire fences bolstered by watchtowers manned by sharpshooters.

The Germans often boasted that no one had escaped from the prison, but the POWs kept trying anyway. Shortly after he arrived, Hoover led one group who dug a tunnel and hid the dirt in the barracks attic. Every day, he felt increasingly confident he would soon break out. But right before the prisoners would have burrowed under the outer fence, the guards caught them in the act. Hoover learned that because of underground microphones, the Germans knew all about the tunnel but let the POWs dig anyway. The guards waited until the very end of the tunnel construction before nabbing the perpetrators simply to magnify the prisoners' misery over their defeat.

With every setback—and he had more than a dozen—Hoover never gave up his quest to escape. One day, he joined a prison detail that used a horse-drawn wagon to collect coal for the stove in their barracks. The coal was stored in a shed beyond the inner fence but within the prison's outer fence. While inside the shed, Hoover's comrades carefully covered him in coal and left. Late that night, he wiggled out of the mound of coal, exited the shed, and climbed over the fence. Thinking he had finally outwitted the Germans, he made a beeline for the woods—and ran right into a startled armed guard. For that failed attempt, Hoover spent two weeks in the cooler—solitary confinement—on a diet of bread and water. In fact, throughout the rest of the year, Hoover became a regular "guest" of the cooler.

By January 1945, the prison population had swelled to 10,000 POWs, causing worsening conditions such as shortages of food and medicine. Seeing waves of roaring Allied bombers heading into Germany's interior, the POWs were convinced that the enemy was losing the war. Most prisoners were willing to remain in Stalag Luft I and wait out the conflict. Hoover wasn't one of them.

One day in early April, he told a small gathering of prisoners, "I've been a POW for fifteen months. That's fifteen months too long. I'm not sticking around for the good guys to show up. If the guards flee before Allied forces arrive, we'll have no protection from the civilians. They hate our guts because of all the heavy casualties they've suffered from our bombing raids. Who knows what they would do to us pilots and crewmen. And think about the SS troops [members of a feared Nazi paramilitary group]. In a last act of revenge, they could storm in here and slaughter us. Also, we have to be concerned with the advancing Russian troops. Yes, they're our supposed allies, but they're unpredictable. They're just as likely to rob or kill us as share their food and vodka. You can stay, but I'm making another try ASAP."

"I'll go with you," said Jerome "Jerry" Ennis, a pilot from the 52nd Fighter Group. Ennis, who had been shot down on his thirty-eighth mission after strafing a munitions train, had spent nearly three years as a POW. A Canadian airman named George chimed in, "Count me in, too."

They came up with a plan approved by the escape committee. A few days later, the trio stood outside the barracks while, on the opposite end of the building, a large group of prisoners staged a fake violent brawl among themselves. As the guards raced to break up the fight, Hoover, Ennis, and George grabbed a long wooden board that they had found under the barracks and ran in the opposite direction to the interior fence. Using the board as a ramp, they climbed over it and then did the same thing with the perimeter fence.

Running through the woods until they were out of breath, they eventually reached the shore of the freezing waters of the Baltic Sea. Because the prison was located on a peninsula, they needed to cross the inlet to the mainland, which was about 700 yards away. They went back into the woods and fashioned a crude raft out of grapevine and fallen thick branches. Because it could hold the weight of only one person, they drew straws. Ennis won.

Hoover and George took off their clothes and handed them to Ennis, who sat on the raft. Then they slipped into the bitterly cold water and, by holding on to the raft while kicking, propelled it to the other side of the inlet before hypothermia (loss of body heat) set in. After the shivering pair put on their dry clothes, they and Ennis ran through more woods until they came to a deserted barn. They spent the night under piles of hay, relieved that they hadn't seen or heard any signs of a search party.

The next morning, they went into a field and ate raw potatoes and turnips. Later in the day, they saw a lone middle-aged German woman washing clothes outside her house. Hoover went up to her and asked, "Do you understand English?" When she nodded, they chatted until he felt he could trust her. He admitted the three of them were unarmed escaped prisoners trying to get to their unit—and they were starving.

Showing her humanity, she made them fried potatoes and eggs. After they wolfed down their first decent meal in more than a year, Hoover asked her for paper and pen, which she gave him. He wrote, "To Whom It May Concern: This lady has been very generous and helped us in our escape.

Please treat her with great kindness." Hoover signed it and handed it to her, saying, "Give this to any Allied soldier you meet."

They thanked her and shook her hand. As they headed down a dirt road, the woman ran out of the house, waving her arms and calling to them. Hoover returned to the woman, who told him, "I read your note." She handed him a pistol and three bullets. "Here. I want you to have this because it will do you more good than it will me."

"Thank you," he said. "You are a very nice person."

Later, near a village, the escapees spotted three bicycles leaning against the wall of a building. "Shall we?" Hoover asked. They hopped on the bikes and rode away. At the next intersection, George said, "I owe you both a lot, and I'm grateful. But I need to make a go of it on my own. Good luck, boys." After shaking their hands, he pedaled off.

Hoover and Ennis headed west, hoping to find friendly forces. What they found instead were Russian troops. Many Russians wrongly believed that any escapee from a German prison camp was an enemy collaborator and, therefore, could be shot or shipped off to Siberia. Knowing this, Ennis, who spoke French, found a French-speaking Russian and fibbed that the two Americans were airmen who had been shot down over Berlin and had been evading the Germans ever since. Believing him, the Russians gave the pair shelter and food.

Two nights later, the pair entered a walled farm compound where about 80 people were huddled. Most were

French citizens whom the Nazis had brought to Germany to toil in forced labor camps. Now that German defenses were crumbling, these workers were trying to return to their homeland. Because Ennis spoke French, they welcomed the Americans.

Later, while the pair slept in the hayloft with many of the refugees, Russian tanks smashed through the wall of the compound. The night air echoed with gunshots and screams. Russian troops then stormed the barn and began killing the people and looting the bodies.

Fearing for their lives, Hoover and Ennis stood against the back wall of the hayloft with their hands in the air, shouting, "We're Americans!" None of the soldiers spoke English or French. Frantically, the two pointed to their own clothes and insignias on their uniforms, showing they were allies. When the invaders finally understood, they let Hoover and Ennis go. As the pair left the compound, they heard more gunfire and anguished screams.

The next day, the escapees spotted a small Luftwaffe (German air force) base that looked all but abandoned. Each of its 30 planes was hidden behind its own tall U-shaped mound of dirt called a revetment and covered with camouflage netting. The planes were Focke-Wulf 190s—the same type that had downed Hoover and Ennis.

Hoover broke out in a big grin. "In prison camp, I often dreamed of stealing a German plane and flying it to safety. Now that dream is coming true."

"Are you serious?" Ennis replied.

"You better believe I am, Jerry. I spent hours listening to Gus Lundquist tell me all about this plane." Before he was shot down and became a fellow prisoner at Stalag Luft I, Lundquist had flown captured German planes in England to evaluate enemy aircraft for the Allies. "From all that Gus told me about the Focke-Wulf 190," Hoover told Ennis, "I think I can fly one—if we find one that's airworthy."

"And fly it to where?"

"Northern Holland, the area Allies have liberated. The Dutch hate the Germans for invading their country, so the people there are on our side. Now then, let's find us a good plane."

Although they noticed several enemy crewmen ambling around the airfield, none of the Germans were carrying weapons, so the pair boldly scurried from one plane to the next, looking for one that wasn't too damaged. But it seemed every aircraft was either pierced with too many bullet holes or was missing a vital cable, wheel, or other part. Eventually, they found one in decent shape, although its wing and tail had been peppered by gunfire. Hoover climbed in and checked the fuel gauge. "The fuel tanks are full!" he announced. "This is the one!"

A mechanic walked warily toward them, so Ennis pulled out the pistol that the German woman had given him and pointed it at him. Learning that the man spoke French, Ennis said, "If you don't help us get this plane airborne, I'll kill you."

Looking scared, the mechanic nodded and hopped onto the wing. Then he reached into the cockpit and jerked on a handle that retracted the tail wheel, causing the tail to slam onto the ground, which damaged the mechanism. Without the wheel functioning properly, the plane couldn't taxi.

Placing the gun against the mechanic's forehead, Ennis cocked the hammer and convinced the German to help fix it. Two hours later, the plane was ready to fly and the engine roared to life. "Okay, Jerry, hop in," Hoover said.

Ennis backed away and shook his head. "No, Bob. After I was shot down, I vowed I'd never get in another fighter plane again. You go ahead without me. I'll take my chances on the ground."

"Well, you better move out fast. Some German trucks are coming this way."

"Good luck, Bob," Ennis said, shaking his hand. "I'll see you in the States. Now get out of here."

Ennis kept his gun trained on the mechanic while giving Hoover a thumbs-up. Fearing the arriving Germans would shoot at the plane if he took the extra time to taxi out onto the runway, Hoover opened the throttle to full power and steered the Focke-Wulf 190 across the grass until it went airborne. He looked down and saw Ennis running into the woods.

For the first few minutes, Hoover basked in pure elation over stealing an enemy plane. But then he felt a new sensation—an extremely disturbing one. *You have to be the dumbest pilot who ever flew,* he told himself. *You're in an enemy airplane with German markings on the wings and a swastika on the tail. You're an easy target for any Allied fighter plane. And you don't have a parachute. Why, you don't even have a map or charts to help you.*

Fortunately, the weather was on his side—overcast at an altitude of 4,000 feet and clear visibility below. He flew right under the clouds so that he could easily disappear in them if any Allied pilots saw him.

Hoover headed west until he reached the North Sea and then hugged the shoreline, hoping to reach the Netherlands before he ran out of fuel. He kept his eyes glued to the ground, looking for windmills, which would indicate he had made it to the Dutch coast. When he was low on fuel, Hoover spotted one windmill, then another. "Yes! Yes! Yes!" he chortled.

Seeing a grass airfield below, he thought about landing there, but decided against it because the Germans were known to mine bases they had used and abandoned. He chose instead to land in an open field. However, when he touched down, he saw a wide ditch that he hadn't noticed from the air. To avoid smashing into it and flipping over, he ground-looped the plane. He swerved so hard that the left wing dug into the dirt and the plane spun halfway around so it was facing in the opposite direction before it came to a rest. The maneuver saved him from crashing into the ditch, but it destroyed the landing gear.

Hoover didn't care. He had flown a stolen enemy plane to safety. For the first time in over a year, he could relax. *I'm free! No more solitary. No more torture. No more hunger. No more humiliation. And no more cabbage soup.* After savoring the moment and his remarkable accomplishment, he eased out of the cockpit and jauntily strolled along a road toward a village that he had flown over a few minutes earlier.

Humming a happy tune, he had walked a few hundred yards when two speeding trucks skidded to a halt in front of him. *Dutch farmers,* he thought. He smiled and waved. But their response was anything but welcoming. Wielding pitchforks, hoes, and shovels, they surrounded him and yelled at him in Dutch.

"I'm an American!" he shouted, raising his hands. "I stole this plane and escaped from Germany." Staring at their menacing faces, Hoover realized that no one spoke English. *I landed in a German plane, so they think I'm from the Luftwaffe.* He had no identification on him. But he did have his dog tags, which he pulled out of his shirt and showed them. "See? American!"

Not sure which side he was on, they kept their pitchforks leveled at him and motioned for him to start walking with them toward the village. Luckily for Hoover, a British army truck rolled by and stopped. "I could use your help," Hoover said to an officer who had stuck his head out of the open passenger side window. "I was a POW but I escaped, stole a German plane, and flew it to Holland. I'm just trying to get back to my forces. These farmers here think I'm a German."

The officer chuckled and said, "I say, old chap. Pop on,

and off we'll go." Addressing the farmers, the officer said in Dutch, *"Alles is goed."* The farmers backed away as Hoover climbed into the cab of the truck.

"What did you say to the farmers?" Hoover asked.

"I told them, 'All is good.'"

"Yes," said Hoover. "All is good. All is most definitely good."

After the war, Bob Hoover, who was awarded the Distinguished Flying Cross, became a test pilot for the military and aviation companies. He then spent more than 50 years thrilling air show audiences throughout the world with his daring aerobatics, often performed in a twin-engine Shrike Commander while wearing his signature business suit and panama hat.

Having flown more than 300 types of aircraft, Hoover was named among the top three aviators in history in the centennial edition of Air & Space Smithsonian. *In 1986, he received the Lindbergh Medal for lifetime achievement and two years later was enshrined in the National Aviation Hall of Fame. The International Council of Air Shows inducted him as their first Hall of Fame member in 1995.*

Hoover never found out what happened to George, the Canadian POW. He also didn't know the fate of his comrade Jerry Ennis until decades later. While Hoover was waiting to perform at an air show in Reading, Pennsylvania, in 1986, an usher said that a man in the audience claimed to be the pilot's old friend from the war and wanted to talk to him. It was Ennis. After sharing a warm embrace, Ennis recalled that after the two bid each other good-bye at the German airfield, he had safely reached Allied forces a few days later. After the war, Ennis taught high school in New Jersey. At the surprise reunion, Ennis got on the public address system and told the air show crowd of 30,000 how he had helped his buddy escape Germany in a stolen enemy plane.

Hoover, who was widowed after 68 years of marriage to his wife, Colleen, had two children, three grandchildren, and two great grandchildren. He died in 2016 at the age of 94 near his home in Los Angeles.

His autobiography, Forever Flying, was one of the sources for this chapter.

"WE LIVE TO FIGHT ANOTHER DAY"

Staff Sergeant Richard "Dick" Morris

Company C, 157th Regiment, 45th Infantry Division, US Army

A violent explosion threw Staff Sergeant Dick Morris and his fellow Allied POWs to the floor of their locked boxcar as their prison train was crossing a stone bridge over the Paglia River in Italy.

The prisoners had just untangled themselves and stood up when another ear-shattering blast rocked their boxcar, knocking them down in a heap once again. "We're getting bombed!" someone shouted. Thunderous explosions left and right battered the train as several boxcars blew up or toppled into the river.

With its doors padlocked, it seemed impossible for Morris and his comrades to escape. He knew the only way out would be if flying shrapnel ripped open a hole big enough for them to flee—as long as it didn't kill them first. Realizing he was likely facing a gruesome death, Morris flattened himself on the floor and prayed, "Lord, spare me just one more time."

He wouldn't have been in this predicament if only he hadn't surrendered to the Germans six weeks earlier. But what choice did he have? Fighting against a superior force would have turned into a massacre for him and the 12 men under his command during that ill-fated patrol.

In the predawn hours of December 15, 1943, near the Italian town of Venafro, the 22-year-old sergeant and his comrades crept behind enemy lines along a 10-foot-wide, 20-foot-deep rocky gully when a German machine gun opened up on them from above. The Americans pressed their backs against the gully wall as bullets rained down on them for hours. At daybreak, the enemy began tossing hand grenades, the blasts hurling shrapnel and shards of rock that ripped into the soldiers.

Trapped and fearing he and his injured men would ultimately perish, Morris made a drastic decision: He would surrender.

Shouting, *"Kamerad, kaputt!"* ("Comrade, it's over!"), Morris scaled the gully wall, and with hands raised, walked toward the German position. Waving a submachine gun and dancing around Morris, an enemy soldier declared in English, "For you, the war is over."

The dozen Americans glumly climbed the gully wall and turned over their weapons. A surge of relief swept over Morris that his patrol was out of immediate danger. But he also felt shame. *The lives of my men no longer depend on my decisions,* he told himself. *I have let down my country.*

As Allied artillery shells exploded nearby, the enemy marched the prisoners to a road where a German soldier was having difficulty starting a captured two-ton Ford truck. Not wanting to die from friendly fire, Morris and his men got the vehicle started and then climbed in the back. "This is the only time today I feel superior to the Germans," Morris muttered to Private John Tourtillotte. "I'm still upset that I ordered us to surrender."

"Hey, at least we live to fight another day," Tourtillotte replied.

The truck took the captives about 40 miles north to the city of Frosinone, where the Germans had turned a former stucco-walled Italian garrison into a POW camp. It housed about 800 prisoners, mostly British soldiers from the 8th Army, along with South Africans, New Zealanders, and Sikhs and Hindus from India. There were only a few dozen Americans.

In the mornings, the POWs received a coffee-like beverage made from water boiled with what looked like burned acorns. The main meal, served at noon, was a tasteless soup with a few green cabbage leaves. On certain days, rice was added. At night, the prisoners received coffee, a loaf of dark bread for every five men, and a one-pound block of margarine for them to divide.

The prisoners voted a British officer named Len as their

leader. Hoping to get the men better food and more of it, he confronted the prison commandant, whom they nicknamed Nugget Mouth because he sported many gold teeth. "We deserve the same kind of treatment that German prisoners receive at the hands of Allies," Len told him.

"Well, you can thank your fellow Allies for our food shortage because they keep bombing bridges and roads, so we can't get food into the prison camp," Nugget Mouth replied. "However, you and your men will soon be on a prison train to Germany where you'll be safe and receive packages from the Red Cross." That was relatively good news for Morris because he figured the train offered the best chance for him to escape.

Christmas came ten days after Morris and his men were captured. The holiday had always been special to him while growing up in Boulder, Colorado. His father was a candy man who made his sweet treats in the back of his store on Pearl Street. "It was a busy time when he earned enough money to tide our family over until Easter," Morris told his comrades. "My dad made dozens of candy canes. Oh, how I loved the smell of peppermint. I had just learned to roll candy canes into an even thickness when I enlisted."

By now, Morris had become close friends with Tourtillotte, 25, who had worked as a machinist at the Bath Iron Works in Bath, Maine. He was a jack-of-all-trades, from cutting hair to sailing ships, from picking locks to performing magic tricks.

Morris and Tourtillotte started making escape plans and took Italian lessons from Private Mike Guele, who was fluent in the language.

Early in January 1944, the POWs were rousted out of their sleep by guards' gruff shouts of *"Raus! Raus!"* ("Out! Out!") The men were herded onto open-air trucks, which sped off in the darkness.

After traveling 90 miles north, the convoy arrived at a new POW camp outside the town of Fara in Sabina. The camp was surrounded by double rows of 15-foot-high barbed wire fencing with lookout towers every 40 yards, each housing two guards, a machine gun, and a searchlight.

About two weeks after arriving here, Morris went to the infirmary with a painful abscessed tooth, but there was no medication available. The German medic handed him a rag to wrap around his jaw and ordered him to bed. The pain eventually subsided, but Morris didn't let the Germans know. He continued to wear the rag because he knew it could conceal a small tool used for an escape.

Days later, the POWs received news that many had been waiting for: A train would take them to a safer prison camp in Germany, which promised better living conditions. But Morris and Tourtillotte weren't interested in another camp. "The train will be our chance to escape!" Morris declared.

He stuck a small folding mess kit can opener inside his cheek, which the rag covered. Meanwhile, Tourtillotte had fashioned a bobby pin from an aluminum spoon and used it to secure a small knife in Morris's thick, wavy hair. He also inserted razor blades and matches inside the bill of Morris's woolen cap.

Before boarding, the 800 prisoners had to strip naked so guards could examine their bodies and clothes for hidden items. When Morris disrobed, his inspector tried to push aside the rag to look into Morris's mouth. Morris howled in fake agony so loudly the German backed off and handed Morris his clothing. The guard found none of the items Morris was concealing.

The prisoners were crammed into dozens of small cattle cars that were eventually padlocked from the outside. Morris and Tourtillotte scrambled aboard quickly to be near their boxcar's one small window, their intended escape hatch. The window was covered with a barbed wire flap held in place by heavy staples on the inside. In the center of the car, the Germans placed a large aluminum chamber pot. Because more than 40 men were jam-packed in the car, there wasn't room for everyone to lie down at the same time.

That night, Tourtillotte began the slow, tedious process of using the knife and can opener to sever the wire flap that covered the window. By 3:00 a.m., he had cut the ends of the wires from the staples on both sides and at the bottom of the window. "We should be able to squeeze our way out once the train slows down," he whispered to Morris.

Just then, the train rolled into a station and jolted to a stop. Guards leaped from the boxcars and surrounded the train. "Quick!" Morris said. "Reattach the wires before they discover what you've done." Tourtillotte frantically slipped the ends of the wires back under the staples.

A guard entered the boxcar and went directly to the window to inspect it. *If the wires don't hold, who knows what the Germans will do to us,* Morris fretted. *Our escape plans will be ruined.* Morris held his breath as the guard struck the wire flap with the butt of his rifle. Incredibly, the wires held. When the guard left, Morris whispered, "Great job, John."

Later that morning on January 28, the train stopped again, allowing the prisoners to stretch their legs and relieve themselves. "One more day in this boxcar will drive me out of my mind," Morris told Tourtillotte. "We've got to make our escape out that window tonight no matter what."

About 1:00 p.m., the train slowed down as it approached the Allerona Bridge, about 80 miles north of Rome. The span, held up by stone arches, had sustained damage from earlier Allied bombing, but, despite missing huge chunks, was still stable—although barely—to handle the prison train.

No one knew that two hours earlier, 27 American B-26 Marauder bombers from the 320th Bombardment Group had taken off from an Allied base on the Italian island of Sardinia. Their mission: bomb the Allerona Bridge.

As fate would have it, the first wave of planes flew over the bridge at the exact moment the train was rolling across it. The airmen couldn't believe their luck. Not only was the bridge undefended, but a German train, probably carrying troops, was crossing it. If the train had been transporting civilians, POWs, or hospital patients, surely there would have been markers on the roofs of the boxcars. There weren't any. The flyboys were about to score a "daily double": destruction of the bridge and a troop train. In four waves, the planes began dropping their load—84 1,000-pound demolition bombs and 36 500-pounders, including some with fuses that delayed the blasts for up to 12 hours.

Morris had dozed off minutes earlier and hadn't heard the loud droning of the approaching bombers. But he jerked awake when flying rocks and shrapnel from the first explosions raked the side of the boxcar. After a short pause, a second round of bombs fell, jolting the entire train, which was now stopped on the bridge. Guards on the boxcars leaped onto the tracks, secured the doors behind them, and sprinted off the bridge, leaving the helpless POWs to face their doom.

A soldier next to Morris thrust his face in the window and screamed at the fleeing guards, "Come back and let us out of here!"

"We're sitting ducks!" Morris shouted as the bridge shuddered and shook from the impact of the bombs. At any moment, he expected his boxcar to blow up or fall into the river.

The men inside were yelling, crying, or praying. Many were banging on the locked doors to no avail. Their shouts were drowned out by the deafening roars from the third cluster of bombs, which wobbled the bridge and train.

Several boxcars were blown to bits and others toppled off the crumbling span.

Another blast tore jagged holes in the roof and the side of Morris's boxcar. Through the smoke and choking dust and other debris, he and Tourtillotte began hustling the smaller men out through the opening. One of the prisoners grabbed the metal chamber pot and used it to break out an even larger section of the weakened wall so others could escape. When it was their turn, Morris and Tourtillotte squirmed through the hole and jumped down onto what remained of the bridge.

An entire 100-foot-long section had collapsed, taking with it several boxcars that had crashed into the rocky, shallow river.

Prisoners in other cars managed to free themselves from their boxcars by squeezing through holes created by shrapnel and flying debris.

Morris and Tourtillotte ran frantically along the trembling bridge. British prisoners from one of the damaged boxcars were sprinting in bare feet. The Germans had taken away their shoes after several Brits had escaped the night before.

Morris scrambled along the rickety bridge framework and jumped about 15 feet down to the riverbed. He landed in an old bomb crater, jarring his entire body. Then the fourth cluster of bombs fell, several making direct hits on the bridge. The blasts blew away the tops of several more boxcars. *Was my boxcar one of them?*

"Dick! Dick! Quit staring at the bridge!" Tourtillotte shouted. "This is our chance to escape! Let's go!" About 150 prisoners were streaming toward the nearby hills as guards stopped fleeing and began firing at them from distant bomb craters.

Near the pair, about 30 POWs were milling around, not sure what to do. A lone German officer menacingly swung his pistol at them and ordered, *"Komm! Komm!"* ("Come here! Come here!") But when a bomb exploded close by, the officer dived into a crater for cover.

Ignoring the German, Morris and Tourtillotte headed north, plowing through the underbrush. They had to clear the area before the Germans regrouped and began rounding up the prisoners.

The pair scampered down a path until they spotted an armed German soldier 20 yards away, talking to a group of Italians. Luckily, the escapees were wearing winter jackets that had been issued the night before their capture. The jackets covered their uniforms so they weren't immediately recognized as American soldiers.

"He's spotted us," Morris said. "Running off will cause him to chase us. We have to walk by him and pretend we're Italian."

As they strolled past the group, they called out, *"Buongiorno!"* ("Good day!") and kept walking, avoiding eye contact. After they were about 25 yards away, the German hailed them by whistling. Pretending they didn't hear him, they kept ambling down the trail. When it turned left, taking them out of the German's line of sight, they sprinted into the underbrush and down a hill, where they hid.

"Well, we live to fight another day," Tourtillotte said.

When it was safe to walk again, they came to a farmhouse. Taking a chance that most Italians sided with the Allies and not the Germans, the two escapees knocked on the door and announced, *"Siamo americani."* ("We are Americans.") The farmers invited them in and said they knew about the bombing of the Allerona Bridge and that prisoners had escaped. In fact, the sounds of blasts from delayed action bombs continued to echo across the valley. Morris and Tourtillotte were led to a large wooden table in the kitchen where, in their broken Italian, they engaged in a stilted conversation with their hosts while eating fresh pasta.

"To sit at a table, to eat from china, to consume hot food, and to sip wine from a glass make Nugget Mouth, sadistic guards, and life behind barbed wire fences seem like a distant memory," Morris said to Tourtillotte.

With their bellies full, the pair slept in front of the fireplace on straw mats. The next morning, the family convinced them to trade their uniforms for regular clothing so they would look like two Italian civilians from a distance. Carrying bedrolls made from their field jackets, the pair traveled north.

Wherever they stayed, the two escapees were treated with kindness. In return, Morris wrote a note for each host to give to any American officer if—and hopefully when—the

Allies captured the area. The note asked that the US government help the family who had paid for food and lodging for the pair.

Morris and Tourtillotte spent two weeks at a large stone farmhouse called Poderina in the Val di Chiana in central Italy as guests of brothers Guido and Giulio Pinzi and their families. The ground floor housed 50 sheep, two oxen, a sow with her litter, and dozens of chickens. The second floor was the residence for the families. As tenant farmers, the Pinzis planted and harvested the crops and took care of the animals and shared the proceeds with the owner of the land, who paid for all the supplies.

Whenever visitors approached the farm, Morris and Tourtillotte were hustled into the grain room to hide. Sometimes, though, the Pinzis would open the door and introduce the escapees to their friends, about whom the brothers would claim, *"Sono gente buono."* ("They are good people.")

After the visitors' departure, Morris and Tourtillotte warned the Pinzis that the more people in the area who knew of the Americans' presence at Poderina, the more perilous it was for the families and the escapees. But visitors still showed up to see the *"americani."*

One day, the Pinzis introduced the landowner's agent to the pair. He wasn't friendly at all and ordered the brothers, "Get rid of them. Germany will win the war."

That night, Morris told Tourtillotte, "It's time to move on. Half the farmers in the valley know we're staying with

the Pinzis. The Germans might pay us a visit at any moment."
Tourtillotte agreed, so the two sneaked out of the house at
4:00 a.m.

They continued northward and stopped at a farmhouse
of tenants on property owned by Il Marchese Antonio Origo
and his wife, La Marchesa Iris Origo. After dyeing the men's
field jackets to make them look more like peasants, the farmers introduced the pair to the marchesa.

Iris, who was in her late 30s, was the daughter of an
American diplomat and an Englishwoman. After she married Antonio, an Italian nobleman, the couple bought a villa,
La Foce, on a large expanse of land and hired 50 tenant
farmers. The Origos funded a school and a clinic with a full-
time nurse for the families.

As Italian war casualties mounted, the Origos estab-
lished an orphanage on the estate for children who had lost
their fathers. Secretly siding with the Allies, the couple also
helped escaped POWs and wounded fugitives who showed
up at the clinic, sometimes even when German officers were
visiting the villa. The Origos engaged in a nerve-racking
balancing act. They had to be nice to the Germans while
covertly assisting the Allies. The couple often endured the
hostile suspicions of Nazi sympathizers who denounced
them to the Germans.

When Germany rushed eight divisions from the north
to battle invading Allied troops from the south, Iris told the
escapees, "It's too dangerous for you to stay here or to keep
going north."

"But we're trying to get back to our unit," Morris said.

"That will have to wait," she replied.

Morris and Tourtillotte returned to the Pinzis, who greeted them with happy tears and open arms. The brothers said when they discovered the two Americans had sneaked out of the house, they were crushed and couldn't understand why it was so important for them to rejoin their outfit. Because everyone in the area assumed the pair had fled, Morris urged Guido and Giulio not to let anyone know the truth.

Rather than stay with the families, the escapees built a sod shelter deep in the woods. They cut down saplings for the frame and for two beds and covered the structure with sod thick enough to keep them warm and dry. From the outside, the hut looked like half of a giant walnut shell. They spent most of their time sleeping in the shelter, viewing distant battles and bombing runs from a ridgeline, and visiting the Pinzis only at mealtimes.

By May, rising anxiety gripped the pair as rumors of Nazi atrocities surfaced: German patrols were abusing women and shooting men in cold blood. Truckloads of enemy soldiers were raiding farmhouses, stripping them to the bare walls. Families were disappearing along with livestock. Germans were crawling everywhere—and they weren't taking prisoners.

Morris and Tourtillotte felt depressed. But their mood brightened when they learned the Allies were battling their way toward Rome. Allied air activity had intensified as fighter planes strafed the area's enemy-held roads several times a week. Leaflets were dropped warning civilians to place white sheets near their homes so that airmen could avoid bombing them. But it left Morris wondering, *Maybe the Germans are putting white sheets around their installations to confuse our bombers.*

Late one day, the nearby city of Orvieto was bombed heavily. Huge explosions lit up the sky for miles. From Morris's vantage point on the ridge, the blasts were spectacular but frightening. Then on June 5, good news spread rapidly from farm to farm: The Allies had broken through the Germans' defense and liberated Rome. By the second week of June, flashes of artillery from both sides became more vivid and the booms from big guns became louder.

As the front drew closer, the escapees' apprehension skyrocketed because they knew that within the next few days, they would be either liberated or recaptured. They abandoned their sod hut and went deeper into the woods, where they watched columns of enemy infantrymen retreating along the trails. "The Germans aren't supposed to be this close to us," Morris said.

He was unaware that the 6th South African Division of the British 8th Army had forced the Germans to retreat to higher ground near where the two Americans were hiding. "There's nothing we can do," Morris said. "We have to stay away from places likely to be chosen as a defensive position by the Germans."

As Allied artillery shells began falling near them, the

pair found themselves in no-man's-land. "We're so close to freedom . . . and capture," Morris told his buddy that night. "What if a passing German patrol finds us? I can't stand the tension. It's unbearable. Don't you feel that way, too?"

Shaking his head, Tourtillotte replied, "You can worry for both of us. I'm going to sleep. Tell me what happens in the morning."

For Morris, sleep was out of the question. Shortly after midnight, two shells passed overhead and exploded above them. The shells had come from German-held territory to the north. *That's a good sign*, Morris thought. *It means the German rear guard has passed through our area. But we're still within range of enemy tanks. We need to move farther down the hill where tank guns can't reach us. To be hit by German fire on our last night of danger would be the worst thing possible.*

Waking up Tourtillotte wasn't easy because the heavy sleeper had snoozed through the blasts. After Morris finally awakened him, his groggy comrade followed him down to a ravine at the base of the hill.

Later that morning, June 17, the sounds of battle had moved farther north. Other than the rumble of Allied vehicles rolling through the valley, all was quiet. "We're no longer in enemy-occupied territory, John!" Morris announced. "The Allies have it now!"

They embraced and then visited the Poderina to say good-bye to the Pinzis. The family, who said the Germans had stolen several chickens during the retreat, prepared one final feast for the Americans—pasta with lamb. For Morris and Tourtillotte, it was a bittersweet meal. They were jubilant to be free, but sad to be leaving this wonderful family.

After dinner, Morris wrote a letter on behalf of Guido and Giulio, extolling their contributions to the well-being and safety of escaped Allied prisoners and praising their steady courage in the face of threats from local Nazi sympathizers. Hoping the military would reimburse the families, he penned a separate letter noting the dates the Pinzis had fed and lodged the two escapees.

As they hugged their tearful hosts, Morris told them, *"Arrivederci."* ("See you later.") But he knew it was really *"Addio."* ("Farewell.")

As the two Americans headed down the trail toward the Allied convoys, Tourtillotte pounded Morris on the back and said, "Well, Dick, we live to fight another day."

Nobody knows exactly how many POWs were killed during the bombing of the Allerona Bridge, although most accounts say at least 400. Ten boxcars were blown apart and many others were derailed or fell off the span. About 200 men were injured. More than 200 prisoners tried to escape, but most were recaptured and sent to POW camps in Germany or German-occupied territory. Only 36 prisoners from the train—including Dick Morris and John Tourtillotte—were known to have safely reached friendly lines.

After the war, Morris spent 35 years teaching high school French and Spanish, mostly in New Canaan, Connecticut, where he raised a family with his wife, Shirley. "I believe that spending six months behind enemy lines where he didn't speak Italian or German really brought home to him the importance of foreign language," said his daughter Sue Finley. "He refused to ever go back to Italy. I think it was just too difficult for him to relive, and so he didn't choose to teach Italian."

Morris died in 2003. He was 83.

Tourtillotte returned to Maine, where he and his wife, Maxine, raised their family in Boothbay Harbor. He died in 1987 at the age of 69.

The original Allerona Bridge was destroyed, and now the only remains are a few stones hidden in the undergrowth. On January 28, 2012, a metal monument and plaque were erected under an arch of the rebuilt bridge to commemorate the victims of the bombing. Morris's family attended along with local officials and representatives from the British, American, and South African embassies.

This story is based on the unpublished memoir of Dick Morris, which was provided by his daughter Sue.

ESCAPE FROM THE LIVING DEAD

Major William "Ed" Dyess

21st Pursuit Squadron, 24th Pursuit Group,
329th Fighter Group, US Army Air Forces

As a veteran fighter pilot, Major Ed Dyess thought he had seen it all. But on April 10, 1942, the day after he became a POW when American and Filipino forces in the Philippines surrendered to the Japanese, he witnessed—and suffered—the first day of a year of barbaric cruelties inflicted by the enemy.

It started with the Bataan Death March, when he was one of 12,000 Americans, along with more than 60,000 Filipino troops, forced to walk for days under relentless brutality and the merciless tropical sun with little or no water, food, or rest. Even before the POWs took their first steps, an American army captain was killed. The enemy soldiers ruthlessly beat prisoners, robbing them of watches, fountain pens, money, toiletries, and personal property.

According to their military code of Bushido (Way of the

Warrior), the Japanese believed surrender was a form of treason, so they treated the POWs as less than human and freely abused, tortured, or murdered them—sometimes just for fun. Many were murdered for being too slow.

During the six-day march from Mariveles, Bataan, to San Fernando, Pampanga, Dyess witnessed much Japanese brutality. Dyess was stunned. *The Japs don't respect human life*, he told himself, using a slur for the Japanese that was common at the time. This sadistic treatment of war prisoners was beyond his understanding. Rage was welling up in him. He felt the urge to sprint up to the closest guard and strangle him. Gradually, Dyess gained control of himself. *By going berserk now, I will only lose my own life without hope of ever helping to even the score.*

He walked past mutilated and crushed bodies—so many that he was no longer shocked.

The heat and misery had numbed his senses, but not enough to keep him from wondering, *Will the next murder be of me?*

When thirst was turning his throat raw, he unscrewed the top of his canteen for a sip of warm water. Suddenly, a Japanese soldier snatched it from his hands and poured the water into a horse's nosebag. After throwing down the canteen, the soldier walked on among the prisoners, swiping their canteens and pouring more water into the bag. When he had filled it, he let his horse drink from it.

Despite the throttling thirst and gnawing hunger, Dyess was spurred on by one motivating thought: *Somehow, some way, I am going to escape. And when I do, I will tell the world about the Japanese atrocities.*

As commander of the 21st Pursuit Squadron for the US Army Air Forces in the Philippines, the Texas-born-and-raised 25-year-old pilot never expected to end up in a death march even after the Japanese had invaded the island country. On December 8, 1941—one day after the Pearl Harbor attack—Dyess headed the first successful air attack on the Japanese in the Philippines. When the enemy pushed toward the capital city of Manila, American and Filipino forces withdrew to the Bataan Peninsula on the southwest corner of the country's main island of Luzon to await reinforcements (which came much too late).

Because of a shortage of aircraft, his unit was temporarily attached to the infantry. Although he and his airmen were ill-equipped and inexperienced in jungle combat, they performed valiantly during the Battle of Bataan in early 1942. A month later, Dyess led his men in America's first amphibious landing of the war, routing Japanese troops at Aglaloma Bay. For his heroism in spearheading the seaborne assault, Dyess received the Distinguished Service Cross.

Returning to the air in his battered P-40 Warhawk he had named *Kibosh*, Dyess commanded a daring raid on the Japanese supply depot at Subic Bay, Luzon, on March 2. In three separate sorties that day, he braved heavy antiaircraft fire to damage or destroy an enemy cruiser, a transport, another vessel, two motor launches, and several small barges. He also strafed warehouses, docks, and shore facilities, inflicting serious damage. For his actions, he received his second Distinguished Service Cross.

When the Bataan Peninsula fell to the Japanese, Dyess's unit was ordered to fly the planes to the safer island of Cebu. On April 9, he refused to abandon those in his squadron who couldn't be evacuated and gave his plane to another fighter pilot for one last bombing run on the way to Cebu. He and his men had planned to fight to the end, but then came the order to surrender.

The following day, the Japanese forced Dyess and tens of thousands of American and Filipino troops on the death march. For six agonizing days and 60 miles, those who weren't murdered for being too slow or didn't die from exhaustion and thirst, trudged under the blazing sun and along roads choked with dust from Japanese convoys. Only once were they fed a fistful of rice and only a few times were they allowed to drink from a filthy carabao (water buffalo) watering hole. One agonizing day, they marched for 21 hours without a break.

An estimated 500 to 600 Americans and 2,500 to 5,000 Filipinos died during the march, which ended at San Fernando, where the prisoners were transported by train to nearby Capas, then marched seven miles to their final destination—617-acre Camp O'Donnell.

The welcome was anything but friendly. Speaking for

the camp's commandant, who was yelling at the POWs, the interpreter told them, "The captain, he say America and Nippon [another name for Japan] are enemies. Always will be enemies. If Nippon do not defeat America this time, Nippon fight again and again until America defeated. Always will be war until America is Nippon's."

In their state of hunger, thirst, and fatigue, many prisoners paid little attention to the tirade. Some actually had their backs turned to him.

"Captain, he say you not prisoners of war," the interpreter continued. "You sworn enemies of Japan. Therefore, you not treated like prisoners of honorable war. Captain, he say you treated like captives, not like soldiers. Captain, he say you will have trouble from him."

With 22 other US Army Air Forces officers, Dyess was assigned to a ramshackle structure 14 feet wide and 20 feet long with an unfinished roof that let in the sun and rain. Because it had neither cots nor mats, the men pulled grass and weeds to lie on in dry weather. When it rained, they crawled under the flooring.

There were no lights in the barracks, although the camp was lit up at night with powerful searchlights atop guard towers spaced along barbed wire fences patrolled by sentries. Escape seemed impossible.

In the early days, the prison had no latrines or other sanitary facilities. Flies by the millions droned for hours, landing upon human excrement and then on the containers of gray moldy rice, which was virtually all the prisoners were given to eat. When the Japanese at last issued shovels for digging latrines, most of the men were too weak to use them.

Dead bodies were lying in and under buildings, out in the open, and in the latrines. Sometimes the men who went out on the burying parties would collapse and die on the spot and needed to be buried themselves.

Starvation was rampant, turning once strong men into living skeletons. While many lost half their weight, Dyess dropped from 175 pounds to 120, leaving every rib visible. On seeing a man lying anywhere, it was difficult for Dyess to know whether the person was dead or alive.

Prisoners suffered from malaria, dysentery, diphtheria, beriberi, and other awful diseases, many borne by the clouds of mosquitoes that ceaselessly attacked the POWs. None of the diseases were necessarily fatal if treated, but the Japanese callously blocked almost all Red Cross shipments of medicine from coming into the camp. Over the next six weeks, an estimated 1,500–2,000 Americans and 26,000 Filipinos died at O'Donnell.

In May 1942, Dyess and most Americans were transferred to a prison complex near the city of Cabanatuan. Conditions here weren't much better than at O'Donnell. The lack of proper food, water, and medicine left POWs looking like the living dead. Despite their weak physical condition, the prisoners were put on various work details such as chopping wood, building paths, and stringing barbed wire. On one 12-man detail, nine collapsed and died. In June and July, nearly 1,300 Americans were buried in mass graves, covered only with a thin layer of dirt.

Dyess was flat on his back for six weeks, ailing from yellow jaundice and dengue fever. Later in the summer, the Japanese accepted a large shipment of medicine from the Red Cross. The boxes contained serum for diphtheria victims, quinine for malaria patients, dressings and antiseptics to treat wounds inflicted daily by the guards, and vitamins to prevent beriberi and blindness. But weeks went by—while hundreds more prisoners died—before the commandant gave permission to open the boxes.

After five hellish months in the Cabanatuan prison camp, Dyess and 900 other American POWs who were relatively the healthiest were sent by ship to Davao Penal Colony on Mindanao, the southernmost island in the Philippines. They arrived November 7, 1942, at Dapecol, as it was called, a sprawling 140-square-mile maximum security prison plantation that held hundreds of hardened civilian criminals, mostly murderers. Prisoners tended to its fruit and nut orchards, vegetable and grain fields, and mahogany forest and farm.

The barbed wire double-fenced perimeter was bolstered by watchtowers, mounted machine guns, guard stations, and nonstop walking patrols. Within the camp, more fences surrounded barracks and other buildings.

In the 10 years of Dapecol's existence, no prisoner had escaped. That's because beyond its fences was an impenetrable, malaria-infected jungle swamp teeming with poisonous snakes, crocodiles, disease-carrying insects, and other menaces. Although the Japanese controlled the island, they occupied only the coastal towns and villages, leaving most of the interior to the indigenous tribes and 25,000 pro-American Filipino guerillas.

When Major Kazuo Maeda, commander of the camp, inspected the scrawny POWs from Cabanatuan, he growled, "I asked for laborers, not scarecrows." To their surprise, he ordered an increase in their food consumption to include pork, beef, cabbage, spinach, squash, onions, potatoes, peanuts, and fruits produced on the camp's truck farms, livestock pastures, and orchards. He also made sure the prisoners had plenty of water for drinking, bathing, and laundry.

Sick POWs were sent to the hospital to recuperate. Guards acted civilly.

Compared to the misery they had endured in their previous prison camps, Dyess and his comrades thought Dapecol was like a paradise. They knew Maeda was being kind only because he wanted them to get into better shape for slave labor. But the humane treatment soon ended. Annoyed that it was taking the men too long to recover, Maeda cut their food intake to rice and soup and put them to work.

Dyess and his fellow barefoot prisoners left the enclosed barracks compound each day to work the land, cultivating bananas, papayas, pineapple, corn, cassava, and other crops. He also cleared jungles and worked barefoot in the rice paddies. His toenails were black from wading in the ooze, and his legs were covered in ulcers and infected cuts.

When their diet was reduced to rice, he and dozens of others fell victim to scurvy, a condition caused by a vitamin deficiency. The inside of his mouth was so blistered and painful that in order to eat he had to throw his head back and drop the rice down in balls, hoping none of them would touch the sides or roof of his mouth.

The Japanese would do nothing for the prisoners. "Major Maeda cries for laborers," Dyess told his comrades, "yet he'll let men like me lie sick and inactive when he could have us on our feet with fruit from the prison plantation or by giving us a few cents' worth of antiseptics." Dyess was eventually cured when his friends fed him papaya, melons, and other fruit that they had stolen from the orchards.

He then came down with malaria, but recovered in January 1943. Days later, he was assigned to drive a cart pulled by a water buffalo. The cart hauled produce and supplies to and from the plantation outside the prison compound. Buoyed by this opportunity, he began plotting an escape plan. He was so convinced he could break out that he sent a postcard to his wife that affirmed, "I will be home."

In February, Dyess schemed with nine other POWs. Captain Sam Grashio, a member of his squadron, had given up a cushy job in the kitchen because he hated the enemy so much he could no longer trust himself with access to butcher knives. Lieutenant Leo Boelens, an Army Air Forces engineer, worked in the prison machine shop, where he could secretly make fishhooks, knives known as bolos, and other items needed for a jungle escape.

The team included three Marine officers, Major Michael Dobervich, a fearless, resourceful tough guy; Captain Austin "Shifty" Shofner, a former football and wrestling star at the University of Tennessee; and Lieutenant Jack Hawkins, a navigation expert who could speak Spanish. Three more were from the army—Major Stephen Mellnik and two sergeants, Paul Marshall and Robert Spielman. Picked to lead the group was Navy lieutenant commander Melvyn McCoy, who at 38 was the oldest and most senior officer.

The plan called for them to slip away from work details in the plantation on a Sunday, when there were fewer guards. The escapees would head north from the camp through the jungle and swamp to a guerilla-held settlement that Filipino prisoners said was only a few miles away. Then they would trek about 75 miles to the island's eastern coast, steal a boat, and sail to Allied territory in Australia, more than 1,000 miles away.

To help guide them through the jungle, they enlisted two Filipino inmates who were serving time for murder. The convicts, Benigno de la Cruz and Victor Jumarong, despised the Japanese invaders and were eager to escape with the Americans. As civilian inmates, they had more freedom outside the barracks compound than the POWs did, so it would be easier for them to sneak out.

The Americans knew that, if caught, they faced a death sentence. But it was a risk all were willing to take because they needed to tell the world about the Japanese atrocities against POWs.

With the help of pro-American peasants, Dyess and his comrades gathered supplies and equipment for their escape. Throughout March, they collected canned corned beef, bolos, socks filled with rice, kitchen matches, first-aid kits with quinine and sulfa drugs, blankets, knapsacks, maps, and money. From a guard, one of the men swiped a compass and a watch that once had belonged to an American soldier. Dyess took Red Cross medical supplies from the prison hospital, leaving fruit as payment. Using a page ripped from a dictionary as his guide, Boelens built a makeshift navigation device called a sextant. They smuggled the items out of the compound in Dyess's cart and hid them in a banana grove near a shack by the fields where they plowed on Sundays.

"We tell no other prisoners of our plans," Dyess said. "It's for their own good. If the Japs discover someone knew about our escape beforehand, his head would be as good as rolling in the sand." The men also agreed not to kill any guards to avoid vicious reprisals upon the entire camp.

Shofner arranged for the three Marines and Grashio to join his plowing detail. McCoy convinced prison officials to let him assemble a work group to construct a shed in the coffee fields—a ruse to get the other six Americans outside the barracks compound.

On Saturday night, April 3, they went over their plans for the last time. They had committed the route and timing to memory. "If our escape ends in disaster, it won't be because of any bungle on our part," Dyess said. "The odds are long but we have to take them." Referring to God, he added, "If the Old Man is with us, we'll make it. If He isn't, we won't."

Sunday morning after breakfast, the Americans split into two details. Shofner led the first group of four, which passed the gate without being questioned and made it to the rendezvous point. McCoy headed the second detail, which included Dyess and the remaining Americans. The two Filipinos planned to sneak out later.

At the gate, McCoy saluted the guard. But rather than wave them through, the guard stepped out into the road and stared at them. *He suspects something,* thought Dyess, who was smuggling some last-minute items. *If he searches me, I'll be tortured and executed. I wonder if he heard my contraband clanking.*

Finally, the guard snapped, "Okay!" He motioned for them to pass. As the men casually walked on, Dyess felt the guard's eyes boring into the back of his neck. Dyess kept waiting for one of the guards to shout for them to stop. But none did. The men made it across the road and disappeared into the tall grass. *The Old Man is with us today.*

They slipped past a guard outpost and continued through the thick foliage to the spot in the plantation where they had hidden their supplies. There, they put on their backpacks and met up with Shofner and the others.

As rain pelted them, they plunged into the dense mosquito-ridden jungle in single file with the two Filipinos leading the way. One man hung back to make sure they weren't being pursued. They plodded in deep mud, trying to follow a barely visible trail as the men took turns going to the front to slash at the tall grass and thorny vines with their handmade bolos. Soon the prickly, sharp vegetation had cut everyone's hands and arms, and leeches had latched onto their ankles.

But to a man, they wanted to forge ahead. "As bad as things are here, we're still better off than at Dapecol," Dyess said.

The path led across jungle streams swollen by the rain. Some were too deep to wade so the escapees chopped down trees to use as bridges. Because the men were weak from malnutrition, they petered out. Late in the day, they halted, having consumed all their water. "I know what to do," said Victor. He pulled down buhuka vines and snipped off the ends. The hollow stems contained pure rainwater, so he held the open end to his mouth and let the water trickle down his throat. Dyess and the others followed his lead.

They pushed on into the night until they came to a raging stream, which they decided to cross in the morning. They cut down trees and branches to build four raised sleeping platforms. After eating cooked rice, they went to sleep, believing the Japanese wouldn't find them in the dark.

The rain stopped, and the jungle grew weirdly silent except for the gushing stream and the whine of dive-bombing mosquitoes. Dyess had just fallen asleep when he awoke to a resounding crash followed by profanity. The Marines' bed had collapsed, dropping them into the ooze.

The next morning, they cut nearly a dozen trees so they could span the stream, which had risen during the night.

Progress was slow and tedious on the other side because of thicker jungle growth. The escapees soon lost the trail. They eventually found tracks and groaned in dismay when they realized that those footprints were their own. Even though they had a compass, they had gone in a wide circle. Hawkins needed to take a compass reading more often—every five minutes—to stay on a northeasterly course toward the guerilla settlement.

Late that morning, they emerged from the jungle and reached the great swamp. They waded into the dark green, smelly water, which became progressively deeper until it was up to their waist. Their feet sank into thick muck. Adding to their woes, mosquitoes and other insects feasted on them, and so, too, did leeches. Towering sword grass, with its sharp blades, continued to slice and dice the men's skin.

Hacking away in the steamy heat and slogging through the swamp drained their energy. By 2:00 p.m., they were too exhausted to continue. They rested on an enormous log that lay across a hammock, a mound that rose a few inches out of the water and supported a stand of trees.

They gathered dry twigs, which Victor used to build a fire for boiling rice and tea in two buckets. Having gained strength from the food and rest, they cut trees for their sleeping platforms when Boelens shouted, "Duck! Duck!" An angry humming sound filled the air. Dyess looked up and saw a huge swarm of bees surging toward him. Before he could react, two stung him in the back with such ferocity he felt as if he had been stabbed.

Dyess dived to the ground and covered his head with his hands, enduring one sting after another. Some of the men plunged into the swamp, while others curled up in balls. No one escaped the painful wrath of the bee attack, which lasted for more than half an hour.

The pain of the stings temporarily took the escapees' minds off their other troubles as they constructed their sleeping platforms. They had no way of knowing how much more swamp they had to wade through. Their bodies were bloodied with countless cuts, which were on the verge of being infected. Their food was running out. They were dealing with leeches. They were exhausted and weak. Some were sick, and others were borderline delirious. Morale had sunk to a new low.

That evening, Dyess thought, *We need a lift. We need some words of encouragement, but I'm not the one to do that. Sam is.* Knowing that Grashio was a devout Catholic and the most religious man among the group, Dyess asked, "Sam, will you say a prayer?"

Dropping to his knees, Grashio led them in the Lord's Prayer, which some of the men didn't know. Then he recited a Catholic prayer called the "Memorare."

"Keep going, Sam," said Dyess.

"Dear Lord, deliver us from our enemies, protect us from disease and the jungle, guide us out of the swamp, and see us safely to the American lines. We ask this in Your name." Everyone responded with "Amen."

The prayers lifted the spirits of the men as they lay

on their sleeping platforms. Before they dozed off, however, they heard mortar and machine gun fire in the distance. "It sounds like a skirmish between the Japs and the guerillas we're trying to reach," Dyess said. "Let's hope the guerillas win."

Feeling more optimistic than ever, Dyess fell dead asleep—until he was jarred awake by a commotion in the middle of the night. Two of the Marines had fallen through their platform and rolled into the swamp again.

On the third day, the escapees continued trudging through the swamp, slashing away at more razor-sharp grass. After two painful hours, they noticed the sword grass was thinner and the water shallower. At 2:00 p.m., they finally stepped out on the other side of the swamp—and now stared at the gloom and slime of the jungle. "It's almost like we're back home," Dyess joked.

The men marched on until they discovered a faint trail leading in the general direction they wanted. Soon Victor, who was in the lead, exclaimed, "Look. Footprints. And they're fresh!" Most of them had been made by split-toed shoes with hobnail heels, which give the feet more freedom on difficult terrain and assist the wearer in climbing trees for sniping. "They could be Jap soldiers or the guerillas."

Three men went ahead on a scouting mission while two stayed behind. The rest went to a clearing, where they spread out their equipment and clothes to dry in the sun.

At 5:30 p.m., the scouts returned. "We found signs of heavy foot traffic and some deserted houses that had recently been lived in," Victor reported. "There's no doubt that the footprints are those of the guerillas. We're close, real close to them."

"And here's some more good news," said Benigno. From his backpack, he dumped out sweet potatoes and plantains, which were then tossed into hot coals and baked. They tasted delicious and boosted the escapees' moods, although the men remained cautious and worried that the Japanese might be lurking in the jungle.

The men chopped down trees, built their platforms, and went to sleep. They were awakened by a loud ripping sound and bitter cursing. For the third time, the Marines had fallen through their bed.

Midway through the fourth day, the path led the escapees to rusty railroad tracks, which they followed until they encountered a patrol from a local guerilla group led by former storekeeper Casiano de Juan, who warmly greeted them once he learned what they had done. He told them they were 12 miles from Dapecol and that the firefight they had heard two nights earlier came from the guerillas beating back a Japanese search party that was hunting the Americans.

From the settlement, the escapees trekked with guerillas through jungles, in swamps, over mountains, and across rivers for four weeks while battling illness, fatigue, and infections. No matter how many of the men were struggling, someone was always strong enough to rally the others. Also spurring them on were their horrible memories of life in the prison camps at O'Donnell, Cabanatuan, and Dapecol.

Ultimately, after 240 treacherous and exhausting miles, they reached the city of Medina on the northeast coast and linked up with American officials.

While the escapees were recovering, Dyess looked forward to telling the world the shocking truth about Japan's appalling, inhuman mistreatment of POWs. When they gained their strength during their stay in Medina, several of the men received new orders to join, on a temporary basis, the American-commanded 110th Guerilla Division in the northern region of Mindanao. Hearing the news, Dyess broke out in a big smile and roared to his comrades, "We are fighting men once more!"

After discovering the escape, Japanese officials punished the POWs in Dapecol by putting them on a barely sustainable diet of rice and salt and banning smoking, reading, and card playing for a month. Also, the prisoners were forced to work the fields only in their underwear to discourage anyone from escaping into the jungle.

Meanwhile, for the next few months, the escapees helped the guerillas in their fight against the Japanese on Mindanao. On July 3, 1943, Ed Dyess, Melvyn McCoy, and Stephen Mellnik were taken by the submarine the USS Trout to Australia, where General Douglas MacArthur, the American field general for the Philippine Army, presented the trio with the Distinguished Service Cross (Dyess's third). Over the next few months, all but one of the escapees made it to Australia and received the same prestigious medal. Sadly, Leo Boelens was killed on Mindanao during a Japanese raid on an airstrip he was helping to build.

The Americans gave detailed accounts to military officials of Japan's horrific cruelty to POWs, but to Dyess's great disappointment, President Franklin Roosevelt and the War Department classified the reports "top secret." Roosevelt and military officials feared that if the story went public, the Japanese would seek vengeance on the POWs or block all Red Cross shipments to prison camps. Another concern was that outraged Americans would demand US forces focus more on fighting Japan than on the current strategy of first defeating the Germans in Europe.

Promoted to lieutenant colonel, Dyess returned to the United States, where he spent two months recuperating in West Virginia. During that time, he told his story to a reporter for the Chicago Tribune, which then battled the War Department for the right to publish it.

Meanwhile, Dyess, now 27, returned to active duty and began flying again. On December 23, 1943, he was on a training mission in a P-38 over Burbank, California, when the engine conked out. Refusing to bail out because he worried the unmanned plane would likely crash into a residential neighborhood, he tried to land on a city street. But a motorist turned onto the street, causing Dyess to take evasion action. His plane then crashed into a vacant lot, killing him instantly. For sacrificing his life to save civilians, Dyess was posthumously awarded the Soldier's Medal. He is buried in a cemetery in his hometown of Albany, Texas.

Just a few weeks after his death, the War Department reversed its policy and revealed to the public the extent of Japanese atrocities. Dyess's firsthand account of the Bataan Death March, his misery in three Japanese POW camps, and his escape was published in a 24-part series in the Tribune, which syndicated it to more than 100 newspapers throughout the country. The series, which is a main source for this story, and published accounts from the other escapees spread throughout the world.

Infuriated Americans demanded the military beef up its operations in the Pacific, which it did with a major offensive in early 1944. The sales of war bonds soared. Japan claimed the stories were nothing more than "vicious propaganda." But with outrage mounting from around the globe, Japan allowed shipments of Red Cross and YMCA supplies to reach the prison camps, and life for POWs marginally improved.

Dyess and his 11 comrades made history by pulling off the only mass escape from a Japanese prison camp during World War II. The War Department later called it "the greatest story of the war in the Pacific."

CROSSING THE WIRE OF DEATH

Lieutenant R. Alex "Andy" Anderson

US Army Air Service, Attached,

No. 40 Squadron, Royal Flying Corps

"**W**ould you like to escape with us?"

Lieutenant Andy Anderson was surprised by the offer coming from three fellow American POWs he had just met shortly after his arrival at the prison camp in German-occupied France. He hesitated answering only because he was relishing the sudden rush of excitement over the chance to break out.

"Come on," urged one of the pilots. "The more the merrier."

Nodding vigorously, Anderson replied, "You better believe I want to escape."

Ever since the 24-year-old aviator had been shot down a month earlier, on August 27, 1918, he had thought about escaping, but he never had the opportunity. He had suffered machine gun wounds to his knee and back from his air battle and had spent several weeks in a prison hospital before ending up at this bleak detention center in Fresnes-sur-Escaut.

The prison had been converted from an old brewery that now confined mostly British servicemen and American pilots under deplorable conditions. Because it had no heating, lighting, or bathing facilities, it was dirty, dark, and dank—and a haven for fleas and rats. Prisoners slept on straw mattresses and received barely enough food to survive.

The offer to escape came after Anderson told his three comrades how he ended up at Fresnes. An electrical engineer who grew up in a well-to-do family in Honolulu, Hawaii, Anderson enlisted in the army in 1917 days after the United States entered the Great War (now called World War I). After flight school, he was sent overseas, where he and several other Americans were assigned to No. 40 Squadron of the British Royal Flying Corps in northern France. He flew an SE5 single-seat biplane with two machine guns, one mounted over the engine firing through the propeller, the other on the top wing that shot over the propeller.

"Four of us had started out on dawn patrol on August thirtieth near Arras," Anderson recalled. "My three chaps dropped out with engine trouble, leaving me in the midst of five hungry German fighter planes. I was taking shots where I could. Then one came headlong at me, and we were both firing away at each other. I thought I was done for, so I decided to slam into him if he held his course. But at the last second, he pulled away. So then, the next plane got on my tail, shooting at me, and I felt the sting of bullets in my knee and shrapnel in my back. I did a half roll and dived trying to dodge these guys. I came out of the dive with just enough room to make a pancake landing. Wouldn't you know, I ended up right beside a German field artillery battery and before I could get out of the plane, the Huns [a term for German soldiers] surrounded me. They took me to a POW hospital in Mons, and when I recovered after three weeks, I was brought here."

"One day in this wretched place is one day too many," said Lieutenant Theose "Tilly" Tillinghast, of the US Army Air Service's 17th Aero Squadron. The day before, the 25-year-old Rhode Island–raised pilot was forced to land his crippled plane near Cambrai, France, after a swarm of German planes attacked him. "I'm lucky to be alive and not so lucky to be captured," he said.

"I wonder how hard it is to break out of here," Anderson pondered.

"Shush," Tillinghast whispered. He pointed to a small box attached to wires that ran across the ceiling. "Be careful what you say. They can listen in on us."

The conversation moved to the prison courtyard, where Anderson learned that the other two American POWs in the group—Lieutenants John Donaldson and Oscar Mandel—were considered by the Germans to be high-risk prisoners.

Donaldson, 21, attached to the Royal Flying Corps's No. 326 Squadron, was an ace pilot, having shot down eight enemy planes. "I paid a heavy price for my eighth kill," he told Anderson. "The Huns shot my plane into Swiss cheese, and I had to make a crash landing near Cambrai. I didn't get far before I was captured." Donaldson was taken to the prison in Condé-sur-l'Escaut, France, where he met Mandel, 23, who had been shot down a few days earlier flying for the US Army Air Service's 148th Pursuit Squadron.

"We didn't stay there long," Donaldson told Anderson. "Mandel and I escaped by jumping out of a second-story window. We landed in the street and mixed in with the townspeople. We made our way at night to an unguarded German airdrome to steal a plane. At dawn, we got the plane in shape to fly. Just then, a German mechanic discovered us and raised a yell. We grabbed him and in the tussle, he stabbed me in the back. It was just a flesh wound. Mandel knocked him out by hitting him over the head with a flashlight. Then we ran for it.

"We passed by seven lines of occupied trenches and hid in a shell hole near the German front line. That night we advanced across no-man's-land and reached a stream, where we peeled off our clothes. We were getting ready to dive in when a Hun patrol captured us. We were brought here to Fresnes and tossed into solitary confinement for fourteen days and given nothing but bread and water."

During their conversation, Donaldson, who had been a student at Cornell University, learned that Anderson was also a Cornell graduate. "I knew there was a reason why I liked you the moment I met you," Donaldson told him. That's when the young pilot asked Anderson to join the others in a breakout.

"How will we escape?" asked Anderson,

"I found a broken saw," Donaldson replied. "We'll break into a locked room on the second floor of the building that serves as sleeping quarters for some of us, including Oscar and me. The window overlooks the back wall of the prison. We'll cut a hole in the ceiling and remove some of the roof tiles, climb out, and jump down. We'll run to the wall, scale it, and, voilà, we're gone."

"But how will we break into the locked room?"

"Another prisoner, a British corporal named George Rogers, will join us. He stole a screwdriver that he'll use to take the hinges off the door."

The plan called for the five to sneak into Belgium, whose border was only two miles away, and make their way to the Netherlands, which was a neutral country. Although Belgium was under German control, most of its citizens were against the occupiers and willing to help the Allies. "We'll have to rely on the kindness of strangers to make it across Belgium and into Holland," Donaldson said.

"I have a miniature compass to help guide us there," Anderson said. "When I was captured, the Huns made me take everything out of my pockets. While the compass was still in my pocket, I hid it in the folds of my handkerchief and then rolled the hankie into a ball before pulling it out. They never examined the hankie."

Over the next three days, the five POWs collected biscuits, crackers, and pieces of bread, which they stuffed in musette bags for their escape.

On the evening of September 26, Anderson and Tillinghast donned flight jackets and slung their bags over their shoulders. They left the barracks, which was in a different building, and joined Donaldson and Mandel in the courtyard.

"Andy and Tilly, to get to our sleeping quarters, we have to walk through the guardroom and up the stairs," Donaldson said.

Scrunching his face in a gesture of skepticism, Anderson said, "It seems risky to march through the guardroom with our musette bags and jackets on. What if they stop us? What if they question us? How do we explain . . ."

Donaldson held up his hand and replied, "Relax, Andy. Just follow my lead and act like you belong in our building."

As the four entered the guardroom, Anderson didn't dare make eye contact with any of the guards. But he didn't need to worry. Two were hunched over a table playing checkers by a gas lantern while the rest were standing around them, watching the game. Whistling a happy tune, Donaldson led the Americans across the room and started up the stairs. *I wish he'd stop whistling,* Anderson thought.

He's going to attract attention. But the guards hardly glanced up as the POWs strode past them.

Once upstairs, they joined Rogers and then sat down and waited in silence for the guards to retire to their first-floor sleeping quarters. Judging by the way they were singing, it appeared it would be a while.

Those Huns are a lively bunch, Anderson thought. *I wish they'd hurry up and turn in.* As the hours dragged on, he could feel the tension tightening his body. *What if someone spots us on the roof? Can we all climb down from the roof without making a noise? If we do get over the wall, won't the villagers see us? Can we really pull this off?*

About 10:00 p.m., the four POWs heard the scraping sounds of the guards downstairs pushing back their chairs. Anderson's heartbeat quickened when footsteps grew louder. *What if the guards come upstairs and demand to know why Tilly and I are here?* But everything quieted down. None of the guards checked on the prisoners.

"Get ready to move," Mandel whispered.

They tiptoed to the room where Rogers had earlier taken the hinges off the locked door to gain entry and then, while standing on a chair, had cut a hole in the ceiling with the broken saw. He had remained in the room, keeping a lookout for any guards. "It ought to be all right now," he whispered. "I've been watching the building next door. They've all gone to bed."

As Rogers was speaking, Anderson glanced upward and

studied the two-foot-by-two-foot opening to the roof. *It'll be a tight squeeze,* he thought.

The others boosted Rogers up into the hole. Then, as quietly as he could, he removed several clay tiles until he could lift himself onto the roof. Gingerly, he crept to the edge and scanned the backyard for guards. Not seeing any, he motioned to Mandel, who emerged from the opening and crab-walked along the sloping roof, the tiles rattling ever so slightly. He froze in a crouch when a guard stepped outside for a smoke. Mandel held that awkward position for ten minutes until the unsuspecting guard returned to his sleeping quarters.

One by one, the prisoners reached the edge of the roof, where they rolled on their sides, dangled from the eaves, and dropped to the ground. As they crossed the backyard, they passed by a guardroom's lighted window and heard movement coming from inside. *They're not all asleep!* Anderson thought. *If anyone comes out now, they'll catch us.* Rather than wait, the five men scampered across the yard to a 12-foot-high cement wall. Earlier in the day, Rogers had arranged for prison workers to pile a mound of dirt against the side, making it easier for the escapees to scale the wall.

Thrilled they had made it this far, Anderson followed Rogers and Mandel, who stayed in the lead because they could speak French and German, although Anderson and Donaldson knew basic French. To their left, houses lined the main street of the village. To their right, running parallel to the street, a canal flowed past the back entrance to the prison. The men reached the canal and swam across it while floating their musette bags on a wooden plank they had found.

About an hour later, a full moon rose over the trees. Anderson stopped to admire its beauty before realizing, *It's so bright it's like the Huns have a giant searchlight aimed at us.* Whenever they reached an open field, they dashed across it.

They soon came upon a bustling, lit-up factory that had sentries posted at various points along its fenced perimeter. Suddenly, about twenty yards ahead of the escapees, a sentry shouted, *"Halt! Wer ist da?"* ("Stop! Who's there?")

Like the others, Anderson dropped to the ground and low-crawled to the shadow of some trees. At any second he expected to hear gunshots as the sentry walked toward them. *"Wer ist da?"* the German called out again.

We're goners, Anderson thought.

Just then another sentry, who was coming up from behind the hiding prisoners, shouted, *"Es ist nur. Peter."* ("It's just me. Peter.")

The two Germans began talking while approaching each other. The first sentry had detected movement, which was apparently Rogers, who was in the lead, but assumed the figure was the other sentry. While the guards chatted, the escapees slipped away.

"We must push ourselves to the limit," Mandel told the

others. "We have to get as far away from the prison as possible."

About 3:00 a.m., they neared a village when, unexpectedly, a dog barked. Then another and another. The five men quickened their pace. By now, it sounded like every dog in the village was howling. A man opened a window and angrily yelled in French, *"Qu'est-ce qui se passe?"* ("What's going on?") Then others popped their heads out and shouted, *"Que diable?"* ("What the devil?")

"The whole town's awake," Anderson whispered to Rogers. "Say something before everyone comes out with their guns."

"Je suis désolé. Je rentre à la maison. Passe une bonne nuit." ("I'm sorry. I'm walking home. Have a nice night.")

Several villagers hurled a few curse words over the commotion and ordered their dogs to quiet down. Luckily, no one came outside, and the escapees continued on their way into Belgium. At dawn, they built a shelter of leafy boughs in the woods near another village.

"Well, I guess we'll find out if it's true what they say about the Belgians helping Allies," said Rogers. While three stayed behind, he and Mandel went up to a house and knocked on the door. Speaking in French, they explained who they were and begged for food from a middle-aged married couple. The husband and wife said they were eager to help the escapees and provided Rogers and Mandel with coffee, bread, and baked potatoes, which they brought back to their comrades.

"I swear this is the best meal I ever tasted," said Anderson after gobbling down his share of the food in their makeshift shelter.

Later, after getting much needed sleep, the five were delighted when the couple arrived at their shelter with a burlap bag of more food and a set of civilian clothes. The group decided that Rogers should wear the clothes because he was a good linguist and had the best chance of faking out officials and enemy soldiers. Anderson was given a civilian cap.

"Be careful," said the Belgian. "Hun gendarmes [German police] are everywhere, patrolling between this village and the next one."

After the couple left, the escapees discovered that their shelter was right by the path the gendarmes used when making their rounds. But as often as they passed by, the gendarmes never knew that five escaped POWs were hiding behind a stack of evergreen branches just a few yards away.

That evening, after walking for a few hours, the men's luck held out when Rogers and Mandel again went to a house where the occupants were willing to assist them. All the escapees were ushered into the kitchen and fed soup and potatoes. The owner brought out a map and showed them where they were. They had meandered for about 20 miles but were actually only five miles from the prison as the crow flies. That meant they were about 120 miles from the Dutch border and safety.

"I know you can only walk at night, so you better get an

early start," their Belgian host said. "By order of his imperial majesty, the Kaiser, no Belgian is allowed in the street after ten o'clock at night. No one will bother you in the villages—except the gendarmes. They stop people all the time for no apparent reason."

Always on alert, the five walked briskly through the streets of the village. It was nerve-racking for Anderson, who thought, *At any moment, a door might open and out will come a Hun.* Several times, they passed Belgians who greeted them with *"Bonsoir"* ("Good evening"), which the men always acknowledged.

Up ahead they spotted the police headquarters and heard several gendarmes outside, speaking German. The well-lit building sat next to a railroad yard. Walking on the other side of parked freight cars to remain hidden from view, the escapees continued their trek. But when their feet began making crunching sounds on the gravel, they tight-roped along the rails or gingerly stepped only on the wooden ties as they passed by the station.

At about 3:00 a.m., weary from trudging through a swampy area in the rain, they reached the outskirts of another town. Pointing to a lone house, Anderson said, "We're all pretty worn out and cold. Let's go and ask them to take us in."

As their interpreter, Rogers balked. "I don't want to wake somebody up at three in the morning." After the others pleaded with him, he and Donaldson pounded on the door while the rest hid behind bushes. Several minutes later, the door opened, and, after a lengthy conversation, Rogers turned around and shouted, "All right, boys, come on in!"

The occupants, a man and his wife, invited them into the kitchen, brought chairs from another room, and let the escapees cozy up to a warm fire in the wood-burning stove. While Rogers entertained the couple with how the men had escaped from Fresnes, the five consumed fresh bread and coffee.

"Would it be all right if we hide in the house during the day?" Rogers asked the hosts.

"Oh my goodness no," the Belgian replied in French. "We don't dare keep you with us. Our house is on the main road that's traveled daily by the Huns. They've stopped here before. It would be unsafe for you to stay. Besides, if they caught us aiding escaped prisoners, our lives would be in danger. You must leave before dawn. But don't despair. This road will lead you to a large farmhouse owned by a good man. I'm sure he'll hide you in the barn for the day."

Out in the mud and the chill of another damp, gray morning, the escapees reached the next house, where the owner reluctantly agreed to hide them during the day in an underground storage cave he had dug into the side of a grass-covered knoll to store food for the winter.

That night, the escapees continued on their way and once again, shortly before daylight, found a compassionate Belgian couple. The husband, a tall, ruggedly built man with a kind face, welcomed them with an offer to assist them any way he could.

"All these years I've been waiting to aid the cause of my country, and now the chance has come," he told them. "You must stay here and keep out of sight during the day. There's a German artillery school just outside this village."

When night came, he brought out a brown suit. "I wish I could clothe you all but this is the only suit I can offer you." He gave it to Mandel, who was closest in size to him.

Over the next two weeks as they hiked across the country, the escapees continued their streak of luck by finding Belgian civilians who provided them with food, clothing, lodging, and intelligence. After they reached the outskirts of Brussels, Anderson, Donaldson, and Tillinghast remained in the woods while Mandel and Rogers, wearing their civilian garb, went into the city to look for a Belgian acquaintance whom Rogers thought would help them get to Holland.

If all went well, the pair would return for the others. But after waiting for more than a day without any word from either one, Anderson said, "We can't stay here indefinitely. Something bad must have happened to George and Oscar. Maybe they were captured. Maybe worse. We need to keep going."

"That's not going to be easy," said Tillinghast. "We don't have civilian clothes, and we can't speak the language. How can we ask citizens to help us?"

"We'll have to count on our high school French," Anderson replied. The next time they approached a Belgian, Anderson said, *"Bonsoir, monsieur. Nous sommes aviateurs americains. Nous avons besoin de votre aide."*

("Good evening, sir. We are American aviators. We need your help.") The approach worked every time.

After nearly three weeks on the run, the trio reached the village of Rauw near the Dutch border. To their everlasting good fortune, they found a kind Belgian in his hardware and bicycle repair shop. The owner, Gustaaf Hus, spoke English. He told them that he and his brother Jan would find a guide to take them into Holland. In the meantime, Jan insisted the escapees stay with him in his large house.

A few days later, two German officers banged on the front door, demanding to see Jan. To avoid detection, the escapees hustled out the back door and entered a ground-level window into a musty cellar. They hid there while Gus received his callers. After the Germans left, Jan gave the "all clear." He told the escapees, "The Germans will be back. About two hundred of them are in town tonight. I've been ordered to provide lodging for twenty soldiers. I'll put them in my stable, but three officers will be occupying a room on the second floor."

"We should sneak out," said Anderson.

Jan shook his head. "The area is full of Huns. I know it's risky, but you're better off here. You must trust me."

He put the escapees in a room on the second floor and then removed the outside knob to make it difficult for anyone to open. Taking their shoes off so they wouldn't make any noise, the trio remained in silent mode for an entire day and night.

The morning of the second day after the officers left the

house, Jan told the Americans, "I just heard that the German authorities are going to do a house-to-house search. You must leave now, but that's okay."

"Why do you say that?" Anderson asked.

Jan broke into a big smile and replied, "Because we found a guide who will take you across the border."

Before the search began the next day, the Americans embraced Jan and Gus and headed off into the night with the guide, who declined to give his name. They slogged through muddy bogs and then rested on a thick mattress of pine needles in the woods during the daylight hours.

"We will reach the village of Bocholt at dusk," the guide told them. "We'll cross a canal by the bridge just after dark when there's no sentry on duty. Then we'll go directly to the Wire of Death."

"What do you mean 'Wire of Death'?" Anderson asked.

"The Huns put up an electrified fence all along the border to keep Belgians from fleeing to Holland," the guide explained. "It carries two thousand volts. Touch it and you'll be turned into a crisp. Sadly, about two thousand have died either by getting electrocuted or by getting shot by the guards. It is important you follow my instructions exactly so you are not, as we say, 'lightninged to death.'"

The high-voltage fence was a mile from the Dutch border that it paralleled. It contained six to eight electrified wires, spaced evenly about one foot above the other and held taut by posts that were ten feet apart. Flanked three yards on either side of the fence stretched shorter non-charged barbed wire fences designed to keep animals and innocent people from electrocution. Guards spaced about 100 yards apart walked back and forth along the fence. At night, the number of sentries doubled—and they were ordered to shoot to kill anyone who failed to heed a warning to halt.

"We will crawl in tall grass to the barbed wire fence, which I'll cut," the guide said. "Then when we reach the Wire of Death, I will snip the four lower strands. The wires are strung so tightly that when I cut them, the tension will yank them away toward the posts on either side of us. We must immediately crawl through, taking care to duck well under the lowest of the uncut wires. There will be another barbed wire fence to get through before we take off and run into the woods.

"As soon as the break in the wire is discovered, the Huns will fire star shells [flares] to light up the area. Should a star shell go up while you're still out in the open, you must dive to the ground and hold your position like an immovable statue until the light fades away. Any questions?"

"Just one. Have you lost anyone?" Anderson asked.

The guide nodded and replied, "Only those who failed to follow my instructions to the letter."

Hours later, they reached the edge of a clearing about 100 yards from the fence. The guide went over to a specific tree and dug into the ground with his hands. He uncovered a pair of rubber hip boots, a pair of rubber gloves, and a wire cutter with rubber handles. "I don't intend to get light-ninged," he whispered.

Because the moon was so bright, they had to wait until the wee hours of the morning before attempting the final push to the Wire of Death. When it was time to go, the guide whispered, "No talking from now on. Follow me."

Tired and stressed, the Americans carefully followed his every move as they slowly wormed their way flat on their stomachs through the long grass. Every few feet, the guide stopped, not moving for a good minute. At various times during these long waits, the exhausted escapees caught each other nodding off. When Anderson fell asleep, Donaldson, who was lying ahead of him, lightly kicked him in the head to wake him up. Later, Donaldson dozed off, prompting Anderson to shake his foot.

The only sounds in the otherwise silent night were the hacking and coughing of the guards patrolling the fence. Anderson wished the grass were taller as a sentry walked back and forth only a few yards from him: left to right, then a minute later, right to left. Suddenly, from about 200 yards away, a shot rang out. The noise startled Anderson, causing his body to jerk so wildly he feared the movement would give him away. He heard footsteps on the run, coming closer and closer. Anxiety forced Anderson to peek over the grass. The guard, who was breathing heavily, shouted to another guard and ran past the prone Americans and toward the source of the gunfire. *Someone else is trying to get across,* Anderson thought. *I hope they make it. I hope we make it.*

Taking advantage of the unguarded section, the guide rose to a crouching position, waved for the escapees to follow, and sprinted to the barbed wire fence. By the time they caught up with him, he had cut the wire. Then they scurried over to the electrified fence.

Snip! Snip! Snip! Snip! With each cut, the wires pulled away in flashing blue sparks. The guide crawled through and frantically beckoned the others. Trying to make himself as low as possible, Anderson exhaled to keep his chest from expanding. As he crawled through, he tried not to think that a horrible death was a few bare inches above him.

I'm through! I'm through! He got up and raced through the cut third fence. Then he sprinted for the safety of the woods, joining his comrades. Tillinghast chuckled and whispered, "I was the last one through the fence, but the first one to make it to the woods."

"We're not safe yet," the guide warned. "We still have a mile to go before reaching the border."

Running wasn't an option because they had to cross a wide expanse of wetlands. They plodded through mud up to their knees, slowing their forward progress. With each passing minute, Anderson could feel his anxiety and frustration rise. Eventually, they made it to solid ground and soon reached a small stream with a plank across it. When they arrived on the other side, the guide told them, "Welcome to Holland."

For the first time in nearly a month, Anderson could relax. "We did it!" he exclaimed. "We successfully escaped Fresnes!"

At daybreak, they arrived in the town of Weert, about

five miles from the border, and celebrated by eating chocolate bars. After buying the incredibly grateful Americans train tickets to Rotterdam, their guide said simply, "Goodbye and good luck."

When they arrived in Rotterdam, the trio went to the United States Consulate, where they had their photo taken under the Stars and Stripes. With his arms around his comrades, Anderson said, "Well, boys, we're once more under the protecting folds of Old Glory."

After the war, R. Alex "Andy" Anderson returned to his hometown of Honolulu, Hawaii, where he raised a family and built a thriving engineering business. But he also found success as a writer of Hawaiian songs even though he had no formal musical training. His first hit was "Haole Hula" in 1927. He went on to write more than 100 island songs, including his most popular one, "Lovely Hula Hands," in 1939, which was recorded by many top singers of his era. He died in 1995, a few days short of his 101st birthday.

When John Donaldson returned to his unit, he was promoted to captain in the US Army Air Service and was decorated with the British Distinguished Flying Cross, the US Distinguished Service Cross, and the Belgian Croix de Guerre. He remained in the military after the war and won the Mackay Gold Medal for taking first place in the army's transcontinental air race in October 1919. He resigned his commission in 1920 to enter the business world and became president of Newark (New Jersey) Air Service, Inc. After winning two races at an American Legion air meet in Philadelphia, he was killed during a stunt-flying performance in 1930.

Theose Tillinghast, who was promoted to captain, remained in the army until 1929, when he joined the Pratt & Whitney Aircraft Company as executive engineer. Later he became president of the United Aircraft Service Corporation. On his retirement in 1958, Tillinghast received the William E. Mitchell Award by the Aviators Post 743 of the American Legion as "the United States citizen making the outstanding individual contribution to aviation progress." He and his wife, Margaret, raised two children and had five grandchildren. He died in 1988 in West Hartford, Connecticut.

George Rogers and Oscar Mandel were captured in Brussels and finished the war in various POW camps. Upon his return to the US, Mandel married and raised a family while enjoying a successful career in real estate. He died in 1970 in Delray Beach, Florida.

It is not known what happened to Rogers.

One of the main sources for this story came from a first-person series of articles that Anderson wrote in McClure's magazine in 1919.

THE PROMISED LAND
Lieutenant George Puryear

95th Aero Squadron, US Army Air Service

Pilot George Puryear was brimming with pride. The lieutenant had just shot down a two-person German plane and, after landing, was about to make them prisoners of war. Seeing soldiers emerging from the woods, he thought they were his comrades, so he waved to them.

But as soon as he heard their voices, his heart sank and his brain told him he was in deep trouble. The soldiers weren't speaking English or French. They were speaking German—the language of the enemy.

He was now the POW. The captor had become the captive.

How could this happen? he wondered while cringing at the weapons pointed at him. *I'm in Allied territory, aren't I?*

Just minutes earlier on July 26, 1918, the World War I pilot was flying his biplane as a member of the US Army Air Service's 95th Aero Squadron. Near Château-Thierry, France, he patrolled over an area where the front battle lines had been shifting back and forth. When he'd taken off that morning, the sector was under control of the Americans. Spotting an enemy plane that had a pilot and gunner, he attacked. After a brief dogfight, Puryear shot the gunner, leaving the German pilot defenseless. With the American in pursuit, the German dived and landed his plane in a field where he dragged his wounded gunner to a nearby house.

Thrilled with his shoot-down, Puryear landed near the enemy plane and planned to capture the two Germans and march them to headquarters. Not until it was too late did he realize the area was once again in German hands. After taking away his flight jacket and goggles, the soldiers led him to the house where he saw that the gunner he had shot was dead from two bullet wounds in the stomach. Yelling at Puryear, the irate German pilot accused him of violating an unwritten aviators' code by shooting at the gunner after forcing down the plane. Puryear denied the accusation, but that didn't stop several soldiers from wanting to execute him.

Never had he felt so helpless and scared. *I'm a prisoner, and they want to kill me!* he thought. *It can't get any worse than this.*

Instead of shooting him, they brought him to an enemy-occupied French village, where a German officer who spoke perfect English interrogated him. Puryear was then transported by train to a prison in Rastatt in southwest Germany, where he was held along with hundreds of French and British officers. The prison was an imposing brick fortress with heavily barred windows.

To fight off his despair, Puryear told himself, *No matter*

how long it takes, I will never quit trying to escape. He soon learned that a POW had used a stolen saw to cut the bottom of an iron bar in a second-story window. Although the bar remained in its normal place, a prisoner could easily move it to the side and squeeze through the window.

Puryear and a French pilot, Andre Conneau, immediately began plotting their escape to neighboring Switzerland, which was neutral during the war. But to reach it, they would need to trek 100 miles through enemy territory. "I have studied the map of this area of Germany so much I can draw it from memory," Puryear boasted.

"Well, I have a good compass and a strong mind to escape," Conneau said. "It should take us anywhere from seven to fourteen days to get to the border."

They collected food for their breakout by eating as little as possible from their daily rations. After lights-out on the night of August 5, the pair tiptoed to the room, carrying their bags of food and a rope made from the sheets of their beds. They pushed aside the cut bar and lowered the rope, which they fastened to a strong bar. Puryear waited for a signal—an owl's hoot—from a prisoner in another room who watched out for the guards.

Hearing the hoot, Puryear squeezed through the opening and began sliding down the rope when suddenly, he heard two hoots—the signal to stop. He quickly climbed up and pulled in the rope just as the unsuspecting sentry strode by below.

"That was a close call," the American whispered to

Conneau. After several tense minutes, Puryear started out again only to hear the double hoot when he was halfway down. *I'm not going back up*, he told himself. He let go of the rope and dropped about ten feet to the ground, lying flat next to the wall while Conneau hauled up the rope. As two guards walked by within a few feet of him, Puryear held his breath, fearing his beating heart was making too much noise. But they didn't notice him. Seconds later, his musette bag, which held his provisions, was lowered on the rope.

Too anxious to stick around for Conneau to drop a blanket for the chilly nights, Puryear sprang to his feet, dashed into the darkness, and waited at a prearranged spot in the nearby woods for his comrade, who showed up an hour later. Five other POWs also made their escape the same way, but went in other directions.

The pair crept through the Black Forest during the night, resting during the day. By the second night, a steady cold rain sapped Puryear, who had no jacket, of his strength. "I wish I had waited for my blanket," he admitted. When Conneau, who wore a fur-lined leather coat, offered to take turns wearing it, the American said, "You are a true comrade who deprives himself in order to share the protection of his coat with me."

"We are in this together," Conneau replied. "You'd have done the same if the situation were reversed."

For shelter from the rain, they snapped off low-hanging branches and made a primitive thatch roof to huddle under during the day. Trying to stretch their meager provisions, they ate little.

Because of the raw weather, Puryear developed a nasty cough, which he tried to suppress, worrying that any hacking would alert the Germans, who were searching for all the escapees. Puryear's feet were sore and blistered, making walking painful. Conneau had brought along Red Cross bandages and used them to wrap the American's feet.

After their third day on the loose, Conneau noticed that Puryear was struggling to keep up. "We still have ten or twelve more days before we reach Switzerland," the Frenchman said. "I don't think it's possible for us to continue like this, unprotected and hurting like you are. If we keep going, you'll die."

Puryear vowed to keep going. That night they pressed on. Though his feet hurt, Puryear didn't complain and tried to walk ahead of his partner. Soon the pain turned into numbness, causing him to stumble frequently.

Near the German town of Baden-Baden, they were startled by an armed German sentry who had popped out of the woods. "Halt!" he commanded, pointing his rifle at them.

Shocked and crestfallen, Puryear and Conneau froze. If they had been in better physical condition, they would have taken their chances by fleeing or rushing the German. But they were exhausted, hungry, and weak, so they didn't put up any resistance.

They were returned to the Rastatt prison, where they

were led into a dank basement and locked up in separate solitary confinement cells for what they were told would be 14 days. Disheartened by his capture, Puryear wondered if or when his parents back in his hometown of Gallatin, Tennessee, and his six older brothers would learn of his fate.

After spending five days in their cells, Puryear and Conneau were transported to a prison camp in Karlsruhe, where they were separately questioned by a German officer about their escape from Rastatt. Puryear answered all his questions truthfully—except how he'd slipped out of the prison. "All I will say about my escape is that no prison guard helped me," he said. A secretary transcribed his answers into a typed report, which Puryear was ordered to sign. Before dismissing him, the officer complimented him, saying, "You are very good at hiding the truth."

"Thank you. I pride myself on being a loyal American."

"Tell me, Lieutenant, what did you do in your civilian life before the war?"

"I earned a law degree from Vanderbilt University and was in my first full year as a lawyer in Memphis when I enlisted in the army the day after America declared war on your country."

"Ah, I see! As a lawyer, you know what to answer and what not to answer."

About a week later, Puryear and six other American POWs were transported by train to the Bavarian town of Landshut, where they were put in a prison converted from a forbidding eleventh-century hilltop castle. Following orders to strip naked, the men were examined to see if they were hiding any maps, compasses, or money. Then they were given prison garb to wear while the Germans took their uniforms to search for concealed items.

That evening, one of the Americans, Lieutenant Batty, showed his comrades a detailed map of Germany. "I had it on me the whole time," he said proudly.

"How in the world did you keep them from finding it on you?" Puryear asked.

"I had it stuck with adhesive tape under the bottom of my foot," Batty replied. "When I stood stripped for the inspection, not even those cunning Huns had the slightest idea that I stood on the map of Germany."

The seven joined dozens of other American POWs who had arrived there weeks earlier. Soon every POW had drawn a copy of the map onto cigarette papers.

Not a day went by that Puryear didn't think about escaping. But the odds of success seemed slim because Landshut was about 170 miles from the Swiss border, the prison walls were thick and tall, and the sentries were always on alert.

However, Puryear learned from a guard that because the prison was becoming overcrowded, some of the POWs would be moved by train to a prison camp in Villingen (now Villingen-Schwenningen), which was only 25 miles from Switzerland. *I have to get on that train*, Puryear told himself. He asked officials if he could be on the transfer list. To his great joy, his request was approved.

When he arrived at Villingen, the prison camp housed

200 Russian officers and 70 Americans in various barracks, which were surrounded by a low barbed wire fence, a four-foot-wide ditch containing an entanglement of barbed wire, and then a nine-foot-tall woven barbed wire fence with a top that curved inward, making it impossible to climb. Patrolling outside this outer fence were sentries armed with rifles and spaced about every 25 yards in an area that was lit up throughout the night, when the number of guards doubled to 100.

Shortly after Puryear's arrival, a guard who was distributing mail told him, "I have good news for you."

"Oh? Did I get a letter from home?" Puryear asked.

"No. For your escape from Rastatt, you had been sentenced to fourteen days of solitary confinement. But you served only five days. Now you must serve out the remaining nine days here." So on Puryear's twenty-fourth birthday, he was locked in solitary confinement again.

After release from his cell, he and fellow aviator Lieutenant Caxton "Tich" Tichenor agreed to escape together, right after receiving their weekly Red Cross food rations. In the meantime, they worked on their breakout with about a dozen other POWs who planned to escape in teams of two or three.

Using wooden slats from under their beds, they secretly built ladders to bridge the fences. They took the boards out one at a time, and, with a smuggled tool, bored holes near the end of each plank and then replaced them under the beds. When it came time to break out, they would wire the planks together while others used a smuggled saw to cut iron bars of several windows. Then they would shove the connected planks out the various windows, drop seven feet to the ground, carry them to the perimeter, place them against the fences, and climb over.

Several prisoners who were staying behind would throw chains made from scrap metal onto uninsulated wires to short-circuit the lights and plunge the camp into darkness. At the same time, a group of Russians would fake a fight in a far corner of the prison to distract some of the guards.

Puryear used prison money to buy from a Russian POW his officer's military overcoat and cap, which looked similar to a German uniform. The American figured if he were disguised as a Russian, civilians wouldn't be suspicious of him because trusted Russian POWs were often allowed to leave the prison for a few hours. Posing as a Russian, Puryear wouldn't be expected to speak German if he were questioned by townspeople. With the rest of his prison money, Puryear bought a knife, a compass, and 20 Papiermark (official German currency at the time) from the same Russian.

On Sunday morning, October 6, Puryear learned that all the Russian POWs were being moved out Monday and that the guards would be inspecting the quarters of all remaining prisoners.

"The Germans will find our planks, wire, and chains," he moaned to his comrades.

"We'll have to leave tonight," Tichenor said. "We can't wait for the Red Cross supplies."

"But some of us are short of food," Puryear said. "I have practically none other than the sugar cubes I've been saving."

Several prisoners who were staying behind donated food to those who planned to escape. Puryear was given four boxes of hardtack (cracker-like biscuits) and an opened can of hash.

At 10:30 p.m., when the barrack lights were turned off, Puryear and Tichenor took out the bed slats and fastened them together with the wire. Donning two layers of long woolen underwear, a pair of pants, two woolen shirts, his Russian cap and overcoat, Puryear draped a haversack containing his supplies over his back.

"Are you ready?" asked a prisoner who acted as a messenger. When they nodded, he said, "Wait until we disable the outer lights. Good luck."

Three minutes . . . six minutes . . . nine minutes. Nothing happened. With his stomach churning from fear, nervousness, and anticipation, Puryear could barely stand the suspense. "When will those darn lights go out?" he mumbled.

Moments later, the lights that had been shining down on the outer fence began to flicker and then went dark. The pair started to feed the connected plank out their window when Puryear spotted a guard standing below the window. They stopped, hoping he hadn't noticed. The guard unslung his rifle from his shoulder and, hearing a disturbance away from the fence, blew his whistle and ran off. Another sentry about 50 yards away remained in place, his weapon at the ready.

"It's now or never," Puryear whispered to Tichenor. They shoved the plank out the window and jumped down to the ground. Just as they placed it against the fence, a guard on the outside perimeter spotted Puryear, who, without hesitation, ran up the board and over the fence while Tichenor hid.

"*Halt! Halt!*" the guard shouted.

Puryear landed on his feet and sprinted for a nearby tree while a second sentry raced toward him. *The only chance Tich has of getting over the fence is if I keep the guards occupied*, Puryear thought. He leaped from behind the tree and began running as the guards yelled and cursed at him. They each shot at him but missed. With no intention of surrendering, he zigzagged to make himself a difficult moving target.

They fired at him again just as he stumbled headfirst into a ditch. Seeing him fall, the sentries assumed they had shot him and turned to chase other escapees. By now the entire camp was in an uproar. Guards were shouting, guns were firing, and POWs were scampering here and there. Puryear got up and dashed toward the woods when a third guard shot twice without hitting him.

Disappearing into the forest, Puryear hustled to an agreed-upon spot where he waited for Tichenor to show up. During that time, he counted about 100 gunshots. A half hour later, everything turned quiet until a bugle blew announcing an assembly of the POWs. *Tich didn't make it,*

Puryear thought. *I'm on my own*. After saying a little prayer, he struck out for the Swiss border alone.

Shortly before dawn, several miles from the camp, he found a spot in the woods to hide during the daylight and ate the hash he had brought. Knowing that when he reached the border, he would have to swim across the Rhine River to Switzerland, he did stroking exercises for a couple of hours.

Monday night—after 21 hours of freedom—he ventured out of the forest and raided a garden of potatoes, cabbages, and turnips. Whenever he was tired, he sucked on a sugar cube to give him energy.

About 4:00 a.m. Tuesday, during a rainstorm, he entered a barn, went up to its loft, took off his waterlogged shoes, and fell asleep from exhaustion. But after only a few hours, he woke up because he was cold. He tried to warm up by exercising his arms and legs, and felt better once his soggy clothes dried out.

Just as the sun was setting and he was getting ready to leave, he heard voices. *Farmers are outside!* he thought. *What if they come inside?* Quietly he moved to the corner of the loft and curled up in a ball. Several farmers opened the barn door and entered. *If they come up here, it's all over. They'll turn me in*. He didn't dare move a muscle. After several stressful minutes, they left the barn. *Thank goodness*. He waited until it was pitch dark before moving out.

Walking briskly, he followed a gravel road and entered the town of Neustadt about 10:30 p.m. He buttoned his

Russian military coat, set his cap down low over his eyes, and walked in a dignified but authoritative manner on the lighted sidewalks.

Soon four young German soldiers strolled toward him. Staying calm, Puryear adjusted his pace so he would pass them when the streetlight shone in their faces and at his back. That way, they couldn't make out any of his facial features. When they neared him, they moved aside, stood at attention, and saluted because they assumed he was a German officer. He snapped a salute back and strode past them without saying a word.

On the next block, he encountered a woman who spoke to him in German, which he didn't understand. Acting like an arrogant officer who had no time for her, he mumbled one of the few German phrases he knew—*"Guten Abend"* ("good evening")—and kept on walking.

Passing by a hotel, Puryear gazed through the windows and saw several German soldiers in the lobby. Seconds later, an officer exited the hotel and began walking briskly right behind him. *I wonder if I can fool him as easily as those soldiers*, Puryear thought. *He's walking awfully fast. I better quicken my pace. I can't let him catch up to me because if he starts talking to me or looks at me too closely, I'm doomed. But I can't walk too fast, or he'll get suspicious.*

Even though he felt sweat from uneasiness trickling down his body, Puryear kept up a staunch military bearing while maintaining a slight distance from the officer. *Why is he following me? Does he suspect something? Does he sense*

I'm nervous? Just as his anxiety intensified, Puryear heard the officer's footsteps fading. The pilot took a quick glance behind him and relaxed. The German officer had turned onto another street.

The next block, Puryear encountered five women heading home from work. They stared at him as they passed by but said nothing. Then a group of male workers headed toward him, so he turned down a dark side street to avoid them.

Leaving the town, he continued along the road, which went up a forested mountain. After about an hour, he reached a clearing that overlooked the town, its streetlights appearing fuzzy and muted by a settling fog. A clock in the town hall chimed the midnight hour. It was now Wednesday. A wave of optimism washed over him and he thought, *I'm going to make it to Switzerland. I just know it.*

Rain started to fall as he continued his trek. As he climbed higher, the rain turned to snow, causing him to slip and fall several times. After hours of difficult hiking, he came to a dead end amid thick underbrush. *Now what do I do? I won't retrace my steps. I have to keep moving forward.* Looking at his compass, he could tell which way was north from the glow of the phosphorus tip of the needle.

But hours of trudging in the cold, the snow, the dark, and the difficult terrain had shaken his confidence and sapped his strength. Now whenever he stumbled and fell, he would lie still for several minutes, dropping off to sleep only to awaken minutes later after hearing an imaginary companion call, "Get up! Get up!" Eventually, Puryear came upon a dirt road and followed it down the other side of the mountain.

Under clearing skies, he rested in the woods throughout the day. Buoyed by knowing he was close to the Swiss border, he ate all but one box of hardtack. At nightfall on Wednesday—his fourth night of freedom—Puryear embarked on the final push. Around 11:00 p.m., he hiked up a hill near the town of Waldshut and, in the moonlight, surveyed a beautiful sight: the Rhine River. He pulled out the little map he had copied in pencil. In place of the name "Switzerland," he had written "Promised Land." He uttered a prayer of thanks to God.

He consumed the last lumps of his sugar and crackers and then studied the fast-moving river. The current would carry him toward the Swiss side, but then a mile downriver, the Rhine curved sharply so the flow would push him away from that shore. *I have to make it across before the current takes me to the bend*, he thought. He knew the river would be freezing and that he had only a few minutes to swim across before hypothermia—loss of body heat—set in. He had heard from fellow POWs about a small cemetery near the Swiss city of Basel that held the graves of Russian escapees who had failed to make it across the Rhine. He also was aware that armed sentries were patrolling the German shoreline.

When Puryear reached the water's edge, he heard a municipal clock bong five times. It was 5:00 a.m. Thursday.

Daylight will be coming soon, he thought. *I don't have time to spare.*

He took off everything except his pants and an undershirt. He put the compass, map, and money in a pocket and tied his shoes around his neck. Setting his eyes on the opposite bank, he said another short prayer and slid into the frigid water.

Although it was breathtakingly cold, he felt good. *I have my liberty. The chance of getting recaptured is past. Either I will soon be on neutral soil and a free citizen, or I will end up in the little cemetery at Basel.* After a few strokes, he realized his shoes were too much of a hindrance, so he tossed them. He swam quietly but swiftly, worried that he'd hear an alarm and become an easy shooting target caught in the glare of a searchlight. But nothing happened.

Soon the swift current snared him and pushed him downstream at surprising speed. This was the moment when he needed all his strength—strength he knew was diminishing by the second from cold and exhaustion. Hypothermia was setting in. He was dizzy and losing a grip on himself. Confused while battling the stiff current, he was no longer sure where he was going: *Am I mistaking the bank I left for the bank I want to go to?* He fought hard to clear his head and regain control of his shivering body. *If I drown, will they put me in the little cemetery with the Russians, or will the Swiss start a new one for Americans?*

Puryear shook off that grim thought and swam with every ounce of effort he had left as the current carried him sideways downriver. He was now within ten yards of the Swiss bank, which, from his perspective, was shooting by him as if he were watching scenery out the window of a fast-moving train.

Finally, his hand scraped the bottom. The water was waist deep, but when he tried to stand up, the current knocked him over and continued to push him. Kicking furiously, Puryear came within a few feet of the bank, but he still couldn't stand up. The current was shoving him toward the big bend in the river, which would take him farther away from shore. *I can't let that happen.* Somehow finding strength he didn't know he had, he swam to shallower water and, while clawing at the bottom, he reached the bank. *I've made it to the Promised Land!*

When Puryear pulled himself out of the water, he couldn't stand up. He was too dizzy, too weary, too cold, too everything to relish the fact that he was in Switzerland. He crawled on all fours like a dog, trying to get his muscles to work. Eventually, he was able to stand up. He then took off his wet clothes, wrung them out, and put them on again.

He staggered to a small railroad house and was greeted by a man whose job was to raise and lower the gates where the tracks crossed a highway. Ignoring Puryear's chattering mixture of French and English, the man took off his own overcoat, wrapped it around the trembling, wet escapee, and brought him inside to sit in front of a fire. The man then brought him a pair of wooden-bottom shoes.

The man still hadn't said a word. It was as if he

understood why this bedraggled stranger had appeared out of nowhere. From a tin pitcher on the stove, the man poured hot goat's milk in a bowl and gave it to Puryear. Nothing ever tasted so good. As the warm milk slid down his throat, Puryear blurted, "*Merci, monsieur, merci.*" ("Thank you, sir, thank you.") The man nodded and spoke for the first time. In German.

Thinking that all Swiss spoke French, Puryear nearly dropped his bowl of milk. *Oh, no! Am I back in Germany? Is he a German sympathizer?* Puryear was seized with dread. His mind raced back to July 26, when he landed in what he thought was Allied-controlled territory only to encounter soldiers speaking German. *After all I've gone through, have I made the same mistake again?*

Fearing the answer, Puryear asked, "Are you Swiss? Am I in Switzerland?"

Seeing the terror on the pilot's face, the man understood what was being asked. Nodding, he replied, "*Schweiz. Ja.*" ("Switzerland. Yes.")

Life again flowed back into Puryear, and he happily gulped down the rest of the hot milk. As the man refilled the bowl, Puryear said, "I am a *Kriegsgefangener* [the German word for a POW], and I escaped. I am an American."

After fixing a breakfast of fresh bread, fried dumplings in gravy, coffee, and goat's milk, the man walked Puryear to a Swiss military post, where a soldier who spoke English provided the escapee with a fresh set of clothes and shoes. Puryear returned the coat and shoes that the kindhearted railroad man had given him. The soldier then took the pilot to the railroad station to catch a train to Bern, where an American official was waiting.

Before boarding the train, Puryear handed the soldier the German money the American had obtained in prison and said, "Please keep half of this to pay for the clothes you gave me and give the rest to the railroad man. I am forever grateful to you both."

When Puryear arrived in Bern, he was greeted by Captain Davis, the assistant military attaché for the region. Davis shook the aviator's hand and said, "Congratulations, Lieutenant. You're the first American military officer to escape from a German POW camp. You should feel proud of yourself."

"Sir," Puryear replied, "the only thing I feel right now is free."

American POWs navy Lieutenant Edouard Izak and pilot Lieutenant Harold Willis, who had escaped from Villingen the same night as Puryear, made it to Switzerland the day after he did. Unfortunately, Caxton Tichenor was caught during the breakout.

Puryear learned that the area where he was first captured had been retaken by the Allies just four hours after he had landed and been surrounded by Germans.

Following his successful prison escape, the army sent

him to various air service units so he could tell his fellow pilots about his POW experiences. After the war, he wrote a first-person account of his escape in the Atlantic Monthly, which provided some of the research material for this story. The same year, he and other former combat pilots performed in air shows across the country, encouraging people to buy war bonds to help pay for the victory in Europe.

Puryear was later assigned to the 9th Aero Squadron based near San Diego, California, where he patrolled the area from the air. While he was flying over El Centro, California, on October 20, 1919, the engine of his biplane conked out. Unable to pull out of a tailspin, he went down with his aircraft, which crashed, killing him instantly. He was buried in his hometown of Gallatin, Tennessee.

THE LONG ROAD HOME

Sergeant John Ransom

Company A, 9th Michigan Volunteer Cavalry

Regiment, Union Army

In the stifling heat of the notorious Andersonville prison camp in southern Georgia, Union Sergeant John Ransom pulled out his frayed diary and stubby pencil and wrote:

> July 8—Oh, how hot, and, oh, how miserable . . . I am gradually swelling up and growing weaker . . . Over a hundred and fifty dying per day now, and twenty-six thousand in camp. Guards shoot now very often. Boys, as guards, are the most cruel. It is said that if they kill a Yankee, they are given a thirty days furlough . . . Water perfectly reeking with prison [waste] and poison. Still men drink it and die. Bread today is so coarse as to do more hurt than good to a majority of the prisoners. The place still gets worse . . . No escape except by death, and very many take advantage of that way.

He set down his pencil and thought about his own attempts at escape. *There has to be a way other than dying,* he told himself. One thing was for certain. He would not give up.

Ransom was determined to return to his hometown of Jackson, Michigan, where, fresh out of school, he had worked as a reporter for the local newspaper, *The Citizen*. However, his career in journalism was interrupted by the Civil War, prompting him to enlist in the Union Army at the age of 19 in November 1862.

Nearly a year later, his unit, Company A of the 9th Michigan Volunteer Cavalry Regiment, of which he was quartermaster sergeant, had joined General Ambrose Burnside's campaign in eastern Tennessee. On November 6, after a fierce 10-hour battle that left 100 of the brigade's troops killed and 400 wounded, Ransom was among hundreds who were captured. The victorious Confederate soldiers stripped them of many of their possessions, including overcoats and boots.

Ransom was forced to give up his blanket. *If I'm going to remain a prisoner of war, I need a blanket or I might die of exposure*, he thought. Hoping to get one by being nice, he befriended a guard who had a warm blanket. After much flattery, Ransom told him, "I'm going into prison at the beginning of a long winter, so could I have your blanket?"

"I like you, John, but not so much that I'd part with it," the guard said. Handing Ransom a canteen full of homemade whiskey, he added, "I'll share my applejack with you, though."

After taking a sip, Ransom said, "I'm carrying a large

sum of money, which after a more thorough search, your fellow rebels will take from me. You're a good fellow, so I'd rather give it to you for your own personal use than have it go to the Confederate cause." He pulled out a roll of "wild eat money"—green paper currency that had no value—and handed it to the guard.

Thinking it was real money, the guard said, "Well, thank you kindly, John. What can I do for you?"

"Let me escape."

"You know I can't do that."

"How about giving me your blanket, because it could save my life."

After some further bargaining, the guard reluctantly handed over the blanket. Ransom correctly figured the rebel wouldn't discover that the money was worthless until long after the prisoners were put in cattle cars for the trip to their prison on Belle Isle, an island camp on the James River across from Richmond, Virginia, the capital of the Confederacy.

Shortly after arriving at the POW camp, Ransom, who had hidden real money on him, bought a large blank book, intending to write a diary during his captivity to pass the time and to give an account of prison life.

In some of his early entries, he wrote:

Dec. 1—A man froze to death last night where I slept. The body lay until nearly dark before it was removed. My blanket comes in good play, and it made the boys laugh when I told them how

I got it. We tell stories, dance around, keep as clean as we can without soap and make the best of a very bad situation.

Dec. 2—Pleasant weather and favorable for prisoners. At about nine in the morning, the work of hunting for [lice] commences, and all over camp sit the poor starved wretches, nearly stripped, engaged in picking off and killing the big graybacks. The ground is fairly alive with them, and it requires continual labor to keep from being eaten up alive by them.

The following month, January 1864, Ransom and fellow prisoner George Hendryx obtained a map of Virginia and two rebel uniforms from a slave working near the prison. The pair planned to sneak off at night, steal a prison official's boat, and row it across the river where a slave would guide them to Union lines. But on the morning of the planned escape, Lieutenant Virginius Bossieux, commandant of the prison, announced at the morning POW roll call, "Some of you are plannin' an escape. As sure as there is a god in heaven, if I catch anyone even thinkin' of escapin', you will be tied up and whipped every day until I get plum tuckered out."

Hearing the threat, Ransom whispered to Hendryx, "This doesn't change a thing. If anything, it makes me more determined to get away."

The two POWs didn't know that they were being secretly watched, so when they went to retrieve their hidden supplies and rebel uniforms, they were grabbed by guards. For punishment, they were "bucked and gagged." For an hour every day for a week, each was gagged and forced to sit in the dirt with his knees up to his chest while his hands were tied to his ankles and a stick was shoved over his arms but under his knees. Also for four hours a day, each man had to carry a heavy log and go back and forth from one end of the prison to the other. If he walked too slowly, guards poked him with a bayonet.

Eventually, the pair and hundreds of other prisoners were shipped in cattle cars to Camp Sumter, a new Confederate POW camp in Andersonville, Georgia, arriving on March 14, 1864. The camp, which soon was called Andersonville, was built to hold 10,000 prisoners.

To Ransom, another prison meant another reason to escape. Within days of his arrival, he, Hendryx, and other POWs began burrowing a secret tunnel. On the night of April 21, after the tunnel reached beyond the prison's wooden walls, several POWs escaped, including Ransom and Hendryx. Running through briar, brambles, and swampy ground together, the pair were scratched up and caked in mud. They had fled three miles from camp when Ransom fell over a log and cracked several ribs. "I can't go much farther," he said, gasping in pain. "You go ahead."

Hendryx shook his head and sighed, "It's no use. You hear those dogs? They're comin' for us, and we're goin' to get caught. I was just hopin' to reach some house and get somethin' to eat first."

Barking with excitement, the dogs soon surrounded

them as five mounted rebels arrived and called off the canines. "You two are fools to think you can get away," the leader sneered at the escapers.

"Well," said his partner, "at least they were smart enough not to keep runnin'." Turning to his captives, he added, "If you had, my dogs here would've tore you to pieces."

After Ransom and Hendryx were escorted back to Andersonville, Captain Henry Wirtz, the camp commandant, cussed them out and put them on the chain gang for two days. The pair realized they got off lucky.

May 16—Two men got away during the night and were brought back before noon. The men are torn by the dogs, and one of them [was] full of buck shot. A funny way of escape has just been discovered by Wirtz. A man pretends to be dead and is carried out on a stretcher and left with the row of dead. As soon as it gets dark, Mr. Dead Man jumps up and runs. Wirtz, suspecting the trick, took to watching, and discovered a "dead man" running away.

Undeterred by their failed attempt, Ransom and Hendryx plotted with others on a massive prison breakout. But on June 10, Wirtz uncovered the scheme and placed dozens of armed guards inside and outside the prison walls with orders to shoot to kill anyone who dared try to escape. Hendryx wasn't fazed. He successfully slipped out in full Confederate dress and got away.

That was the only good news. For those in Andersonville, every day brought bad news—mostly about death. The prison eventually held more than four times its capacity. The overcrowded conditions, little food, inadequate medical care, and poor sanitary conditions led to thousands of deaths from malnutrition and disease for roughly 30 percent of the prisoners.

June 26—They die now like sheep—fully a hundred each day. New prisoners come inside in squads of hundreds, and in a few weeks are all dead. The change is too great and sudden for them. Old prisoners stand it the best . . . No wind or breeze to blow away the stench, and we are obliged to breathe and live in it. Dead bodies lay around all day in the broiling sun, by the dozen and even hundreds, and we must suffer and live in this atmosphere. It's too horrible for me to describe in fitting language.

As his physical condition worsened, Ransom was transferred in September to the Marine Hospital in Savannah, Georgia, where his health improved considerably, although he still needed a cane to get around.

Three weeks later, after a brief stay at a prison camp in Millen, Georgia, Ransom and other POWs were put on another train for Blackshear, Georgia. Each of the two doors of his crammed boxcar were opened slightly and guarded by two rebels. *This is my chance to escape,* he thought. After squeezing past his fellow prisoners, he reached one of the doors and began talking with the guards.

At about 3:00 a.m., after the train had gone over a bridge spanning the Altamaha River near Doctortown, Ransom took a deep breath and leaped through the open door into the darkness, not knowing where or how he would land. He hit the ground hard and rolled down a high embankment. A guard fired a single shot but missed. To Ransom's relief, the train didn't stop.

Overcome by a joy he hadn't felt since his initial capture, Ransom sat on the ground with his back propped up against a big pine tree. *I'm out from under rebel guard!* he thought. *I hardly know what to do with myself.* He was so happy that he ignored the bruises and scratches he suffered from his jump. What he couldn't ignore was hunger.

A day later, Ransom, still wearing a rebel jacket, encountered an elderly slave who was working on a fence post on a plantation. After Ransom explained he was a Union soldier who had escaped, the slave brought him a tin of rice, cold yams, and fried bacon. "My master would whip me within an inch of my life if he found out what I had done," said the slave.

Despite the risk, the old man showed up the next afternoon with boiled seasoned turnips, corn bread, and milk. "Oh, this is so good," Ransom gushed. "This is the first milk I've had in a year."

"I beg you, sir, to go off in the mornin'. I'm wary of gettin' caught helpin' you."

"I'll leave. Thank you for your kindness."

"I'm prayin' the war gets over, and the Yanks free all us slaves."

The next day, Ransom headed north, but tripped and

sprained his ankle. Staying deep in the woods because rebels were everywhere, he suffered the next three days without
any food other than a piece of stale corn bread he had saved
and a raw potato.

Just before dark on the sixth day of his freedom, he spotted a house and watched it for more than an hour. The only
person he saw in the fading light looked like a black woman.
Assuming she was a slave who would help him, he knocked
on the door. He was surprised when a white woman, who
had a dark complexion, answered.

"I'm a rebel soldier who was sick in the hospital, and now
that I've recovered I'm tryin' to return home," he said in a
fake southern drawl. "I'm hungry. Can you spare somethin'
to eat?"

"Why of course," she said. "Come in and sit down while
I fix you supper."

She politely asked him questions, which he answered
with various lies. She told him that her husband was a
Confederate soldier who had been killed in a battle near
Atlanta. Throughout their conversation, she kept going in
and out of the kitchen, where a black slave boy was helping
prepare the meal. At one point, Ransom noticed the child
riding off on a horse. *I wonder if I just walked into a trap,* he
thought. *Well, if I did, I hope I get a whack at that supper
before I'm hauled away.*

The woman was extremely polite and continued convers-
ing with Ransom. About an hour later, he began hearing
barking dogs. He looked at the woman and saw guilt painted

on her face. *Yep, my freedom is over,* he thought. Minutes later, six large bloodhounds bounded through the open back door and began sniffing him.

The woman began to cry. "I knew you were a Yankee from the start," she admitted. "So I had my slave boy send for the home guards in Doctortown. I'm sorry."

"I understand why you did it," he replied grimly. "You need not make a scene over it."

Five horsemen arrived, dismounted, and four of them came in with guns cocked. "Good evening, gentlemen," Ransom said.

"Good evening," said the leader. "We're lookin' for a run-away Yankee prowlin' 'round here."

"Well, you needn't search any farther," Ransom replied. "You have found him."

"Before you take him away, allow me to serve y'all supper," said the woman. The men accepted her invitation. While they ate, Ransom told them about his initial capture, imprisonment, and escape attempts.

When it was time to leave, the woman handed him a bundle that included a shirt, stockings, and a chunk of dried beef. On the horseback ride to Doctortown, Ransom was disappointed but not depressed. *I'll try to escape again at the next opportunity,* he thought.

A week later, on December 11, Ransom and two thousand other POWs were put on a train bound for Charleston, South Carolina. They rode on 40 open platform cars, each with six guards. During the trip, he made fast friends with

POWs Dave Buck and his cousin Eli Buck, who both belonged to the 6th Michigan Volunteer Cavalry Regiment. Wearing rebel jackets, they had been escapees for nearly three months and were in sight of Union lines when they were recaptured.

The trio made a pact that they would jump off the train together at the first chance they saw. Late the following night, when the train neared Savannah, Georgia, Dave woke Ransom and Eli and whispered, "The guards have nodded off. Now's the time." He leaped from the open car, followed by Ransom and Eli. Awakened by the movement, the guards opened fire. One bullet knocked off Ransom's cap and another grazed Eli's arm, but that didn't stop the escapees. They kept running through the swampy woods. Fortunately for them, the train kept going.

They eventually encountered an elderly slave woman, who quickly guessed they were Yankee runaways. "No need to worry," she said. "I won't tell. I'm your friend. And as a friend, I must tell you that you don't want to keep goin' the way you're goin'. Not more than twenty rods [100 yards], there's a rebel picket [guarded outpost]." Pointing to the opposite direction, she said, "About thirty rods that-a-way, there's a shed. You hide there, and I'll fetch my brother. He'll know what to do."

Trusting the old woman, the men did what they were told. About an hour later, her brother, whose name was Major, showed up with a tray of boiled turnips, corn bread, and smoked bacon. "I've been forced to work, shorin' up the walls on rebel forts outside of Savannah in preparation of the comin' of the Yankees," Major said. "There's a fort south of here in bad shape. I think I can get you through the line before mornin' to a safe hidin' place."

The plan called for the escapees to reach the Ogeechee River, which was about eight miles west of Savannah, and wait for General William Sherman's Union troops, who were routing the rebels during a bloody march from Atlanta to the sea.

About midnight, the escapees followed Major through turnip patches, hedges, woods, and swamps until they neared a picket of a few dozen rebels who were asleep. "Follow me and be really quiet," whispered Major. He guided them through the picket as the escapees gingerly stepped around and sometimes directly over the sleeping men.

Shortly before dusk, the four rested at the edge of a swamp. "I have to leave you and go work on the fort, but I'll find someone to guide you," Major told them. "Just stay put."

As it grew lighter, the sounds of rebel drums and bugles playing reveille filtered through the woods in all directions. "We must be surrounded," Ransom said.

"Don't fret," Dave replied. "We'll make it to our lines."

Ransom's legs were aching, and he walked with a limp. By the time the new guide led them on a three-mile trek to the slave quarters of a plantation, Ransom was struggling to keep up. Welcoming the arrival of the Yankees, the slaves fed them until their bellies were full. Before the next push toward the Union lines, Ransom told the Bucks, "I'm all tuckered out and hurting. You better leave me with these friendly slaves and go on ahead to our lines."

"Nonsense," said Dave. "You're comin' with us."

A slave then took them to another plantation about three miles away, where they learned that Union gunboats were anchored off the coast near the mouth of the Ogeechee. Wanting to reach the vessels, the escapees hopped into a borrowed dugout canoe at midnight and headed down the river, which was lined with pickets along the banks.

Seeing rebel campfires glowing in the woods by the river, Ransom whispered to his comrades, "We're going right into the lion's mouth." Unexpectedly, their canoe got caught up in the unseen branches of a submerged dead tree. The boat wobbled and pitched everyone into the cold water. Ransom managed to hang on to his diary and blanket, but most other supplies floated away or sank.

While Ransom and Eli clung to the hung-up canoe, Dave swam ashore and asked a slave from a nearby plantation for help. Using another boat, the slave rescued Ransom and Eli and brought them to shore. "It's a good thing you got snagged," said the slave. "Not more than a mile downriver, you'd have run right into a blockade of rebel boats."

Realizing they couldn't reach the Union vessels, Ransom and his comrades decided to follow the slave's advice to seek help from a certain Mr. Kimball, a white Southerner who had assisted runaway slaves and Union escapees. He lived 15 miles away.

Battling bad colds, sore throats, and constant fatigue,

the trio set off through the woods toward Kimball's residence. Several times along the way, they had to hide after spotting Confederate infantrymen marching on the roads. "It's getting harder and harder to move during the day without being seen," Ransom complained.

On the sixth night since their escape, they came to a guarded canal that was lit up by strategically placed campfires. "We have to get across before daybreak," Dave told the others. They chose a spot to cross where a lone cavalryman was riding his horse back and forth near one of the canal's locks (solid gates used to raise or lower the water level).

Timing his move when the mounted guard had his back turned, Dave scampered across the skinny top of the lock and reached the other side. Then, after the rebel completed another pass, Eli made it swiftly and quietly across.

I'm so slow I'll be caught for sure, Ransom thought. *But I have to try.* For the first time since he had jumped off the train, he was scared. Waiting for the right moment, he hobbled onto the lock and tried to maintain his balance as he worked his way along the top. Ransom was about halfway across when the rebel turned his horse around and began heading toward him. *If he shoots me, he shoots me*, Ransom thought. Rather than freeze, Ransom wobbled toward the other side until he reached it safely. The rebel gave no indication that he saw the Yankee.

About noon, the threesome neared a house and watched people going in and out—a white middle-aged woman, a teenage girl, a boy, and three black boys. "Somethin' tells me she's a Union woman," said Dave.

While his comrades stayed hidden in the bushes, he knocked on the door and chatted with the woman. A few minutes later, he returned with bread and dried beef. "I was right," he said. "Her name is Mrs. Dickinson, and she said for us to lie low until late in the afternoon in case visitors come." Twice over the next few hours, Confederate soldiers made brief visits.

Around suppertime, the trio entered the house. At first, Mrs. Dickinson's teenage daughter was afraid of the men. "I ain't never seen a Yankee before," she admitted. After staring at them, she declared, "Why, Mama, they look just like everybody else."

They had taken off their blankets and other wraps and enjoyed a dinner that the two women prepared. Afterward, Ransom wrote a letter and handed it to Mrs. Dickinson. "This letter is directed to the officer commanding the first Yankee troops who show up here," he explained to her. "It tells him all the good things you've done for us runaway Yankees." Just then they heard horses approaching. He looked out the window and warned, "Two rebel officers are coming!"

The escapees bolted out the back door and hid in the woodshed, where they could hear the officers say they had come to pay the daughter a visit. "Who was runnin' out the back way?" they asked. Before the daughter could answer,

Mrs. Dickinson replied, "That was my brother Sam and his slave hurryin' back home."

"Oh, we thought it might be one of your suitors," one of the officers said to her daughter. After an hour's visit, they bid the daughter good night and said, "We'll send some men to guard your house—and keep your suitors away."

As soon as the rebels left, the escapees gathered their things and continued toward Kimball's house. When they arrived there the next day, he shook their hands and said, "I'm mighty pleased to meet your acquaintance. What's mine is yours, except what's mine ain't much."

Kimball, a white-haired, stoop-shouldered gentleman in his 60s, told them, "Even though I'm a Georgian, I'm a Union man. All five of my sons were drafted into the rebel army, and all refused to serve, so two of them were executed, another is in prison, and the other two fled. The rebels know I'm true blue to the Union and have thrown me in prison time and again. They've stolen my livestock and destroyed much of my property, so I've had a hard time of it. But I hear General Sherman is on the march, and glory be to God, the old Stars and Stripes shall wave over my house soon!"

After serving them a big meal, he guided them to a safe place to hide near the banks of the Ogeechee. He also gave them a ham, sweet potatoes, corn, coffee, an ax, and a butcher knife. They cut down small trees to build frames for a shelter and covered it with overlapping palm fronds. All they had to do now was wait for Yankee forces to thrash the enemy.

With food, fire, and shelter, they were relatively comfortable. The men were concerned that smoke from their fire could attract the rebels, whose voices were easily heard as Confederate boats traveled down the river. Although there was a chance retreating rebels would stumble upon the trio's camp, Ransom wasn't too worried. "Rebels are too busy fighting the Yankees to bother looking for us," he said.

The following morning, Dave crept out of the shelter to see if he could learn anything about the advancing Union soldiers. About an hour later, he returned and told the others, "I talked to a slave, who said Yankee scouts had been seen near the bridge up yonder, so the main army is expected any day. The rebels will fall back across the river and contest the crossin'. With Confederate fortifications from here clear down to Savannah, expect some hard fightin' to take place. Savannah is the pride of the South, and they ain't easily goin' to give it up."

The next day, as the sounds of combat grew louder and nearer, Ransom wrote in his diary:

Dec. 22—Considerable firing up in vicinity of the bridge. Can hear volleys of musketry, and an occasional boom of cannon. Hurrah! It is now four o'clock by the sun and the battle is certainly taking place.

Later—Go Sherman, we are listening and wishing you the best of success . . . Give 'em another. That was a good one. We couldn't be more excited if we were right in the midst of it.

Hurrah! . . . If we had guns, [we] would go out and fight in their rear [and] surround them.

On the morning of December 23, the three men, who'd had little sleep because of the fighting during the night, left their shelter, wondering if their fellow Yankees had won the battle. "We must be very careful now and make no mistake," Ransom said. "If we run into a rebel squad, we'll likely get shot."

When they neared a road, they could hear troops marching toward the river. While Ransom and Eli remained hidden, Dave crossed a rushing stream and crept closer to see if the soldiers were Union or Confederate. A few minutes later, he returned and, from the other side of the stream, shouted, "Come on, boys! They're Yankees!"

Ransom and Eli had to cross a log over the 15-foot-wide stream. Eli had no trouble, but Ransom slipped and fell into the water. He saved his diary but lost his blanket, which had kept him warm from his first day in captivity until now, the last minutes before rejoining the Union side. After a tiring struggle, he reached the bank and climbed out. "If the water had been another foot deeper, I would have drowned," he told his comrades.

When the three emerged from the woods in front of the 80th Ohio Infantry, they didn't get the initial reception they were expecting. Seeing three scruffy, shaggy-haired men in tattered rebel garb, the startled Yankees leveled their weapons at them. The escapees held up their hands while Dave quickly explained who they were. The scowls on the troops' faces turned to smiles, and they rushed up and shook hands with the former POWs.

Although Ransom was cold and wet, he didn't care. After 14 grueling months, he was finally safe. Two days later, on Christmas Day, Ransom was riding on a supply wagon when he recognized his old Michigan unit approaching from a side road. Ransom leaped off the wagon, ran in front of the men, and began jumping up and down and waving his arms in happiness.

Leading the Michigan troops was Lieutenant Colonel George Acker. Because he didn't recognize Ransom, who now weighed only 95 pounds and had yet to clean up or change into a Union uniform, Acker angrily yelled, "Get out of the way, you lunatic!"

Still smiling, Ransom responded, "I'm no lunatic, sir. I'm Sergeant John L. Ransom of Company A, Ninth Michigan Cavalry. Merry Christmas!"

Once members of his unit realized who John Ransom was, they embraced him and told him they had received a report he had died in Richmond ten months earlier. He was even given a funeral back home.

After the war, Ransom returned to Jackson, Michigan, and went back to work at the Citizen. *At the urging of editors, he published his diary in a series that ran weekly in the* newspaper. In 1881, the series was published as a book, Andersonville Diary, which became a popular and widely acclaimed account that has been used by Civil War researchers ever since. It is the main source material for this story.

Ransom married and eventually moved to Chicago, where he worked for the Merganthaler Linotype Company before settling in California. He died in 1919, at age 76, and is buried at Mountain View Cemetery in Los Angeles County.

ABOUT THE AUTHOR

Allan Zullo is the author of more than 120 nonfiction books on subjects ranging from sports and the supernatural to history and animals.

He has introduced Scholastic readers to the 10 True Tales series, gripping stories of extraordinary persons who have met the challenges of dangerous, sometimes life-threatening, situations. Among the titles in the series are several books about combat, including *D-Day Heroes*, *Heroes of Pearl Harbor*, *Vietnam War Heroes*, *World War I Heroes*, *World War II Heroes*, *War Heroes: Voices from Iraq*, and *Battle Heroes: Voices from Afghanistan*. Among other books in the series are *Young Civil Rights Heroes*, *Police Heroes*, *FBI Heroes*, and *Heroes of 9/11*.

In addition, Allan has authored five books about the real-life experiences of young people during the Holocaust—*Survivors: True Stories of Children in the Holocaust*, *Heroes of the Holocaust: True Stories of Rescues by Teens*, *Escape: Children of the Holocaust*, *We Fought Back: Teen Resisters of the Holocaust*, and *10 True Tales: Young Survivors of the Holocaust*.

Allan, the father of two grown daughters and the grand-father of five, lives near Asheville, North Carolina. To learn more about the author and his books, visit his website at www.allanzullo.com.